An Adventure in Healing & Wholeness

JAMES K. WAGNER

An Adventure in Healing & Wholeness

The Healing Ministry of Christ in the Church Today

UPPER
ROOM BOOKS
NASHVILLE

Unless otherwise designated, scripture quotations are from the New Revised Standard Version, copyright © 1989 by the Division of Christian Education of the National Council of Churches of Christ in the United States of American, and are used by permission.

Scripture quotations designated RSV are from the Revised Standard Version of the Bible, copyrighted 1946, 1952, and © 1971 by the Division of Christian Education, National Council of the Churches of Christ in the USA. Used by permisson.

KJV is used to identify quotations from the King James Version of the Bible.

Any scripture designated AP is the author's paraphrase.

Excerpts from *Blessed to Be a Blessing* by James K. Wagner. Copyright © 1980 by The Upper Room®. Used by permission of the publisher.

"An Experience in Imaging Prayer" by Matthew H. Gates. Used by permission of the author.

Excerpts from *Letters on the Healing Ministry* by Albert E. Day. Copyright © 1990 by The Disciplined Order of Christ. Used by permission.

Prayer from "Service of Word and Table IV" from *The United Methodist Book of Worship*. Copyright © 1992 by The United Methodist Publishing House. Used by permission.

Excerpt from *Disciplines 1982*. Copyright © 1981 by Upper Room Books™. Used by permission of the publisher.

The cover logo design is by Janet Murray. The moving lines at the base of the illustration suggest the adventure in healing. Healing is a moving process. The boldness and turbulence of these lines imply the tumult that many go through while healing. The circle depicts the joy and strength a person experiences when he or she becomes a whole person in Christ.

Cover design: Bruce Gore
Third printing: 1999
ISBN: 0-8358-0689-8

The Upper Room® Web Site: http://www.upperroom.org

Printed in the United States of America on acid-free paper

To all—
who are obedient,
intentional, and joyful
about the healing ministry
of Christ in the church today.

CONTENTS

Preface

~~~~~~~~

Welcome to *An Adventure in Healing and Wholeness*. An adventure can be an undertaking of uncertain outcome, an exploration of the unknown, or an exciting experience. I commend you for being adventurous enough to explore the healing ministry for yourself and for the church today. My prayer for you is that the Holy Spirit will have some pleasant and life-enhancing surprises for you.

The purpose of *An Adventure in Healing and Wholeness* is to provide a basic guide, an elementary workbook, a fundamental understanding of the healing ministry of Christ in the church today. This text is designed specifically for those in the church who are curious as well as those who are ready to explore and experience healing and wholeness ministries.

A special word of appreciation to Janice Grana, Editor/Publisher of The Upper Room, for her personal encouragement, her support in committing Upper Room resources in developing healing ministries, and her assistance in securing a study leave for me to complete the research and writing of this book. The editorial assistance of Lynne Deming and Rita Collett is also acknowledged with thanksgiving.

I express gratitude to my mother, Lillian Wagner, for providing quiet space to write and for her consistent, lifelong witness to prayer power and Christ-centered faith.

To my colleagues in healing ministry and to the hundreds of congregations and church leaders in Australia, South Korea, South Africa, Sierra Leone, and the US who helped to shape this publication, I am deeply thankful. You have overwhelmingly affirmed the practicality and authenticity of *An Adventure in Healing and Wholeness*.

James K. Wagner
Nashville, Tennessee
January 1, 1993

Introduction

~~~~~~~~~~~~

Are any among you sick? They should call for the elders of the church and have them pray over them, anointing them with oil in the name of the Lord, . . . so that you may be healed.

—James 5:14, 16

God uses medicine, hospitals, and various psychotherapies to bring healing, but these resources alone are insufficient to meet our total health care needs. Some religious observers are predicting that by the year 2000 the majority of churches in each community will be offering active, effective healing ministries. The churches will not replace the healing professions and medical sciences, but more and more Christians will seek the best medical care and the best spiritual care combined.

Today Christ is calling the church to reclaim and to offer healing ministry along with teaching, preaching, and discipling ministries. Indeed, the local church is a primary healing community. Evidence supporting this view is coming increasingly from the health care professions that frequently do not address the spiritual dimensions of the healing process.

David Hilton, M.D., and former staff member of the Christian Medical Commission (World Council of Churches), is convinced that

the most important dimension to health is the spiritual. Even in the midst of poverty some people stay well, while among the world's affluent many are chronically ill. Why? Medical science is beginning to affirm that one's beliefs and feelings are the ultimate tools and powers for healing. Unresolved guilt, anger, resentment, and meaninglessness are found to be the greatest suppressors of the body's powerful, health-controlling immune system, while loving relationships in community are among its strongest augmenters. Those in harmony with the Creator, the earth, and their neighbors not only survive tragedy and suffering best, but grow stronger in the process.[1]

An Adventure in Healing and Wholeness is a carefully designed and field-tested introduction to intentional local church healing ministries, developed by The Upper Room staff to meet the growing need for a biblical, balanced, wholistic, authentic approach.

This educational, experiential focus combines information and formation, the inseparable twins of Christian spirituality. The goal is to receive more information about healing and wholeness while being formed in the mind and spirit of Christ.

The publication of this workbook edition of *An Adventure in Healing and Wholeness* was motivated by increasing requests from churches for practical resources in healing ministry. It is intended for private study and reflection as well as for group study and discussion sessions.

Another way to experience *An Adventure in Healing and Wholeness* is to invite a guest leader, who has been trained and certified by The Upper Room, to lead a weekend event in your church. The curriculum consists of six workshop sessions covering the material in the first six chapters of this workbook and concludes with a Service of Holy Communion and Healing. To schedule a guest leader for your church contact:

Director of Healing Ministries
The Upper Room
P.O. Box 189
Nashville, TN 37202-0189

A Word about Workbook Use

~~~~~~~~~~~~~~~~~~~~~~~~~~~~~~~~~

For Use with Group Study

One person may serve as the leader/coordinator throughout the study, or group members may share leadership from session to session. Each chapter concludes with a "Group Reflection/Discussion Guide" designed to encourage sharing and to facilitate additional learning experiences.

Group leaders need to be flexible, using only what is appropriate to their groups. Do not feel you must use all of the group suggestions.

Raise these questions for group consideration at each session:

~ What insights or questions came to you during your reading of this chapter?

~ What were some of your thoughts and feelings as you reflected on the material and topics?

~ What actions or changes did this week's study prompt you to make in your life? Be specific.

To foster group ownership in this learning/growing experience, invite the group to covenant:

~ to be present for all sessions as much as possible. Let the group decide on meeting dates, times, location.

~ to pray for one another daily.

~ to read and study the assigned chapter in preparation for each meeting.

~ to give permission to express disagreements in an atmosphere of mutual support.

~ to come to each group meeting with a loving heart, an open mind, and a teachable spirit.

Your shared times together are special times to discover the mind and spirit of Christ in your midst. Whether you are studying this book privately or in a group, saturate each session in prayer. Allow the focus of your prayers to arise from the felt needs and life situations of the moment. Pray as the Spirit leads you.

For Individual Use and Study

I encourage all readers to do the "Personal Reflection" exercises, outlined in each chapter. Consult the "Group Reflection/Discussion Guides" for additional suggestions.

~~~~~~~~~~

As you now prepare to launch out on *An Adventure in Healing and Wholeness*, take to heart this word of encouragement and caution from Albert D. Day, a pioneer in healing ministry during the 1950s:

> *Blessings on you who are seeking to follow in the footsteps of Jesus and to fulfill his command to heal the sick in his name and through his name and through his power. Keep humble. Hold sacred the confidences entrusted to your keeping. Be patient with those who need to come again and again. Guard against the intrusions of well-meaning people who have an unenlightened zeal for God and whose too readily volunteered testimony and exhortation are the source of endless confusion. Let no current skepticisms daunt you. Not everyone will experience the specific healing he or she is seeking, but many will. However, each one will be blessed and helped in some way. Be alert to discover in the unhealed or in their environment or in yourself any hindrances to the renewal of life and seek to clear them away.*
>
> *This ministry requires constant self-examination and ever larger dedication. Whatever else you do, keep on loving those who need you, those who oppose you, those who fail you. If necessary, lose your life for their sakes and for Christ. So doing you will find life for yourself and for your people on deeper levels. You are Christ's missioner and he will never fail you or your people![2]*

A Prayer for the Guidance of the Holy Spirit

~~~~~~~~~~~~~~~~~~~~~~~~~~~~~~~~~~~

Come, Holy Spirit, enlighten my mind, cleanse my motives, clarify my intentions and guide my ambitions, especially in this matter and mystery of healing.

When full understanding is not possible,
*   give me faith to trust in you anyway.*
When my questions are greater than my answers,
*   give me faith to trust in you anyway.*
When my doubts outweigh my certainties,
*   give me faith to trust in you anyway.*

Above all else, Holy Spirit of the Living God, decrease my desire to live in my restrictive world of self and increase my desire to live in the freedom of your kingdom.

In the name of the One who makes possible the answer to this prayer, in the name of Jesus, I offer this request.
Amen.[3]

Chapter One

An Overview
of the Healing Ministry

~~~~~~

BEGIN BY TAKING THE TRUE/FALSE QUIZ below, and then list some of your personal questions about healing ministry. This exercise will provide a focus for study and a forum for discussion and reflection throughout *An Adventure in Healing and Wholeness.*

True/False Quiz

1. Every local church automatically has a healing ministry. (T / F)

2. We can translate the New Testament Greek word for our English word *salvation* as *health* or *wholeness.* (T / F)

3. God's intentional will for all human beings is to have good health in body, mind, spirit, and in all human relationships. (T / F)

4. Every prayer you and I pray is an act of healing and wholeness. (T / F)

5. Most church members are enthusiastic about the healing ministry and want their pastors and priests to conduct public healing services in their churches. (T / F)

6. Before beginning healing services in the church, we want to be certain that someone in the church has the Holy Spirit's gift of healing. (T / F)

7. Anointing people with oil when praying for healing is taught in the New Testament. (T / F)

8. The laying on of hands is an expression of compassion and love. (T / F)

9. When Jesus healed people, he used only one method. (T / F)

10. Death is the ultimate healer. (T / F)

What are some of your questions about the healing ministry of the church? List them below.

Key to True/False Quiz
(indicating where each statement is discussed within this workbook)

1. True. See Chapter One, page 19.
2. True. See Chapter Two, page 28.
3. True. See Chapter Seven, page 108.
4. True. See Chapter Seven, page 121.
5. True *or* False. See Chapter Seven, page 113.
6. False. See Chapter Seven, page 109.
7. True. See Chapter Six, page 100.
8. True. See Chapter Six, page 99.
9. False. See Chapter Two, page 28.
10. False. See Chapter Three, page 54.

As we continue this healing ministry overview, let us consider the basic nature of the church, the body of Christ, by discussing the first statement in the True/False Quiz:

Every local church automatically has a healing ministry.

The correct answer is *true*. Some people will answer this statement only on the basis of whether or not their church has a stated time and place for healing services. However, a public healing service is only one kind of evidence that points to healing opportunities in the life of the church. Yes, every local church is engaged automatically in healing ministry even though it may not have a public healing service.

Here is a sampling of the scriptural authority given to the church for engaging in all of the ministries of Jesus Christ.

Matthew 4:23
Jesus went throughout Galilee, teaching in their synagogues and proclaiming the good news of the kingdom and curing every disease and every sickness among the people.
(See also Matthew 9:35.)

Persons often quote this verse to summarize the threefold ministry of Jesus: teaching, preaching, and healing. Although Christians have no doubt that Jesus engaged in all of these ministries, some persons question whether the followers of Jesus can offer these same ministries effectively—especially the one on healing.

John 14:12-15
Very truly, I tell you, the one who believes in me will also do the works that I do and, in fact, will do greater works than these, because I am going to the Father. I will do whatever you ask in my name, so that the Father may be glorified in the Son. If in my name you ask me for anything, I will do it. If you love me, you will keep my commandments.

This is one of the most mind-boggling, spirit-stretching passages in the New Testament. Not only does Jesus proclaim that each of his disciples is expected to do the same works (ministries) as he did; he also says that Christians will do greater works (enhanced and ever-expanding ministries). Why? Not for their glory, but for the glory of God whom Jesus most often called "heavenly Father." Then in verse 15 Jesus adds an affirming, yet challenging word: *I expect you to carry out all of my commandments, not because you think you are able, but simply because you love me.* (AP)

Matthew 28:18-20
Jesus came and said to them, "All authority in heaven and on earth has been given to me. Go therefore and make disciples of all nations, baptizing them in the name of the Father and of the Son and of the Holy Spirit, and teaching them to obey everything that I have commanded you. And remember, I am with you always, to the end of the age."

In his final words and parting instructions before ascending to heaven, Jesus reminds the believers to teach the new followers "to obey everything that I have commanded you." This would include his clear mandate to love one another and to keep on teaching, preaching, and healing.

Plus . . . Jesus added the amazing promise: *And don't ever forget, you are not alone. I am with you always, even to the very end.* (AP)

Matthew 18:20
For where two or three are gathered in my name, I am there among them.

Hebrews 13:8
Jesus Christ is the same yesterday and today and forever.

The last three scripture passages highlight several important spiritual principles, especially related to healing ministry:

First, Christians are not "orphans" or "loners" in ministry. Even though Jesus is no longer in his physical body, his risen, eternal presence is with us forever.

Second, wherever Christians gather in the name of Jesus, his spirit is in that gathering.

Third, whenever Christians claim his presence, he comes with all of his ministries (teaching, preaching, and healing).

Fourth, as in the administration of the sacraments (Holy Baptism and Holy Communion) the worship leaders represent the Christ but are not the Christ; so it is in healing ministry. Those who engage in compassionate prayer for others are representing Christ as the healer.

The primary tasks of those who offer healing ministry are to be obedient to Christ and to show compassion for others. Think of those

20

who pray for others as friends of Christ who intentionally care about all of God's children, pointing not to themselves but rather to the healing Christ.

Personal Reflection
~~~~~~~~~~~~

Look again at the five scripture passages quoted above, taking each one separately:

- ~ Invite the Holy Spirit to open your whole being to God's special word for you.
- ~ Read the passage aloud several times.
- ~ Allow the scripture to "sink in" and to resonate with you.
- ~ Record below any thoughts, feelings, insights, or questions that may arise.

- ~ Thank the Holy Spirit for this special time of centering and being spiritually formed by God's word.

In our generation, the church is rediscovering the ministry of healing. Today Christians (lay and clergy) who minister in the name of Jesus Christ are helping many people in their quest for good health.

The healing ministry, a powerful witness to God's love and compassion for all persons, is an effective way in which the Holy Spirit touches us to make us whole in body, in mind, in spirit, and in our human relationships. As one Christian said it so well, paraphrasing Matthew 4:23:

Preaching proclaims the gospel.
Teaching explains the gospel.
Healing makes real the gospel.

Whenever and wherever two or more persons meet in the name of Jesus Christ, he is present, bringing benefits and blessings beyond measure. His spirit is with us in every worship service, Bible study, prayer group, and Christian fellowship gathering. One of the goals of this workbook is not only to help readers appreciate and acknowledge the presence of Christ in the body of Christ but also to help them move ahead in offering healing ministries with more intentionality. Let us be more definite in naming various expressions of healing ministry that are happening already in our local churches and in developing new forms of ministry that facilitate personal contact with and openness to the healing Christ.

Personal Reflection

Think about all the ministries that are happening in your local church. List in the left column those you would put in the category of helping, caring, healing ministries. In the right column name some types of healing ministry that your church might consider in the future.

Present Healing Ministries   *Future Healing Ministries*

Continuing our overview, we need to be sensitive to reasons why some Christians are negative toward, and have serious questions about, the healing ministry.

1. Some have had personal experiences with unethical, dishonest, self-styled, charlatan faith healers.
2. Some who watch healing services on television receive two falsely perceived messages:

    ~ that healing ministry primarily deals with physical illnesses;
    ~ that all healing services in the churches are copies of television-type healing services.

3. Some are threatened by those who show emotion in public. Some would say it is okay to be emotional at the ball game but not in church. The real threat is not emotion but emotionalism—the manipulation of emotions to achieve a certain purpose.

4. Some have a very private kind of Christianity and are not comfortable sharing their faith or their personal problems with others.

5. Some have the notion that if medicine and psychology cannot cure them, they are incurable. Religious help and spiritual therapy are irrelevant, according to many.

6. Some in our churches believe that God worked healing miracles in the early days of the Christian movement, but that God does not dispense these special signs and wonders in modern times. The Holy Spirit, according to some, acted in these unusual ways only in the New Testament era (as in the Book of Acts) to establish Christianity in the world. This attitude is sometimes called "dispensationalism."

7. Some sincerely believe that sickness is God's way of punishing or disciplining us for our sins. Jesus did not understand illness in this way.

8. Some believe that no supernatural agent or power can change human beings or situations. Some would say, therefore, that prayers of thanksgiving and praise are appropriate, but that prayers of petition and intercession are ineffective and meaningless.

9. Some Christians do not take seriously the spiritual world, even though an estimated fifty percent of the New Testament deals with spiritual phenomena such as:

> *God, kingdom of heaven, prayer, evil, demons, angels, spirits, Holy Spirit, unseen forces, mysteries, miracles, spiritual gifts, spiritual fruit, spiritual rebirth, and so on.*

10. Some in our churches are afraid of the healing ministry. They express this fear in many ways:

   ~ fear of the unknown
   ~ fear of uncertainty
   ~ fear of not being in control
   ~ fear of failure
   ~ fear that the congregation is not ready

Consider this response by a Presbyterian pastor in Ohio to those who say that conditions are not right for a healing ministry.

> *Not everybody tithes, but we still take an offering every Sunday morning. Some are ready to tithe; some are not. Likewise, some are ready for a healing ministry; some are not.*

Perhaps we can sum up these ten attitudes on the part of some Christians in three words: *misinformation*, *apathy*, and *skepticism*.

Keep in mind and in prayer that knowing Christ's healing presence and enabling power in our lives does not come after we have answered all the hard and difficult questions. Rather, we experience Christ's adventure in healing, wholeness, and salvation by taking risks for him, by having trust and faith in him, and by obeying him.

During the last half of the twentieth century, the healing ministry of the church is being roused from generations of slumber. This global initiative of the Holy Spirit is unprecedented in church history. In scope and movement, this renewal and rediscovery of Christ's ministry of healing is international, intercultural, interracial, and interdenominational.

Christ is calling us to reclaim and to offer his healing ministry, along with his teaching and preaching ministries.[4]

Group Reflection/Discussion Guide

Chapter One: An Overview of the Healing Ministry

~~~~~~

1. Give group members an opportunity to share their personal questions and concerns related to healing ministry (page 21). Do not attempt to give easy answers or to solve the difficult problems that might surface. Rather, create an atmosphere of listening, caring, and loving that will prevail throughout *An Adventure in Healing and Wholeness*.

2. Examine the ten reasons why some Christians are uncertain about the healing ministry (pages 23–24).

   ~ Invite someone in the group to read aloud all ten.
   ~ Ask whether any of the group members relate
     personally to any of these. Ask that they be specific in
     their answers.
   ~ Name additional attitudes that block healing ministry.
   ~ Consider some helpful ways to deal with:
        skeptical Christians
        apathetic Christians
        misinformed Christians

3. Discuss ways to offer a positive understanding of healing ministry:

   ~ Outline a strategy of educational/experiential settings
     and opportunities that your local church could offer.
   ~ Given your church's organizational structure, how
     might the group members take action on these
     educational/experiential suggestions? Keep notes in
     the workbook for later reference.

4. You may want to pray this prayer in several group meetings. Invite the group members to pray in unison:

   Spirit of the living God, whose healing presence
   we now seek and claim, we lift up to you
        our questions and answers,

our doubts and affirmations,
our stories of failures as well as successes.
As we covenant together,
may we learn from one another,
may we be totally receptive
to your wisdom and insights,
may we eventually emerge
with a better understanding
of your gracious healing ministry.
And in this learning, growing process,
grant each of us wholeness in body, mind, spirit,
and in all our relationships.
In the name of Jesus Christ, we pray. Amen.[5]

Chapter Two

A Wholistic Understanding of Health

~~~~~~

JESUS UNDERSTOOD AND DEMONSTRATED the relationship among physical health, mental health, and spiritual health. The salvation that Jesus offered included, but went beyond, spiritual well-being. Because Jesus loved the whole person, his goal was to help each person become whole. The Gospel accounts of Jesus' life and ministry illustrate the truth of this last sentence again and again.

Matthew 9:1-8 is the story of the man on a stretcher, whose friends brought him to Jesus. Before Jesus healed the man physically, he dealt with the man's spiritual condition: "Take heart, son; your sins are forgiven."

John 5:1-15 is the account of a man who had been paralyzed for thirty-eight years. Before Jesus could heal the man physically, he had to work with the man's negative attitude: "Do you want to be made well?"

Because Jesus understood the complex nature of human beings, he did not give everyone the same kind of help or the same kind of therapy. Some people he physically touched in the healing process; some he did not touch.

Some he prayed with silently; some he offered a spoken word. Some he helped by visiting in their homes; others he healed without making a house call.

With some he mentioned the faith factor; with others he did not. Even people with the same illness sometimes received different therapies. For one blind man, he applied a mud cake; on another nonsighted person he did not use mud cake therapy, he simply spoke words of healing.

Why? Because each person is uniquely different. Let us learn a valuable lesson from Jesus and be sure that we do not get in a rut, mechanically proceeding to give the same therapy to everyone with similarly diagnosed illnesses or problems. What works for one person may not work for another.

Jesus used many methods and a variety of therapies in order to heal the whole person. The answer to statement 9 in the True/False Quiz is *false*. Jesus was not a cookie-cutter healer.

The healings performed by Jesus give witness to God's intention of restoring wholeness to all people and to all creation. The healing ministry of Jesus testifies to the spiritual power upon which God builds the kingdom and on which believers can base their lives. When Jesus gave the ministry of healing to his disciples, he intended Christians to serve as instruments through which God's healing can flow, God's wholeness can be realized, and God's salvation can be completed.

The Greek word *sozo* has several implications and meanings when translated into English. *Sozo* can mean "to save," "to heal," or "to make whole." The answer to True/False Quiz statement 2 is *true*. Knowing this, we can say that salvation not only means the rescue of the soul or the spirit but also the reality of wholeness wherever brokenness exists. In a sense, the church's total ministry is a healing-saving-wholeness ministry to broken spirits, hearts, minds, relationships, and communities in a broken world.

Yes, our English words *health*, *wholeness*, and *salvation* stem directly from this same Greek root word. Think of Jesus not only as Savior but also as the One who enhances your health and makes wholeness possible in body, mind, spirit, and relationships. The word *wholeness* derives from *holism,* meaning to emphasize the organic or functional relationship among parts versus a segmented, disassociated approach to life and human nature.

To illustrate the various ways English translators of the New Testament have rendered the Greek word *sozo*, read Matthew 9:20-22. We find *sozo* (in the original Greek) three times in this passage.

English Bibles	Sozo translated
The King James Version (KJV)	"made whole"
The New International Version (NIV)	"healed"
The New Revised Standard Version (NRSV)	"made well"
The Amplified Version	"restored to health"

We now move to a working definition of health and wholeness. Health in the biblical sense is not simply the absence of disease. Your doctor may pronounce you "disease-free," but you still may be unhealthy. Think of health in terms of wholeness, balance, and harmony in your life (your body, your mind, your spirit, and your relationships). When one or more of these areas becomes unbalanced, it influences and affects your entire being.

One pastor described the process this way:

Germs do not cause disease. Germs are agents of disease, not the cause. Disease has its roots in an imbalance in our lives. Disease has its roots in the disintegration of the wholeness of our lives.

This disintegration blocks and obstructs the natural healing energy that constantly seeks to flow through our lives. This disintegration of wholeness makes us vulnerable to disease to which we would not otherwise be susceptible.[6]

In other words, when the immune system of our physical being gets out of balance, we get sick.

Personal Reflection

~~~~~~~~~~~~~

What personal experiences can you recall that relate to the pastor's statement above?

To help visualize human nature wholistically ponder this concept:

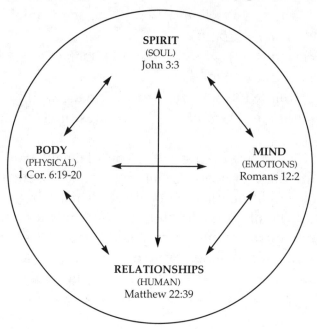

The circle represents one human being. Write your name in large letters inside that circle. When you look at that circle, think of yourself. Inside the circle is everything that is you:

~ a body or a physical self

~ a soul or a spiritual self

~ a mind or an emotional, thinking, feeling self

~ relationships connecting you with others and with your world

You may have a healthy body and a healthy mind, but if you do not have a healthy relationship with God or if you cannot get along with other people, then you still lack total health and wholeness. The double-pointed arrows symbolize interactions and connections. The arrows remind us of the impact and influence that each area of our being has on our total being.

When we consider our total being, we realize that the state of our spiritual health impacts and influences our physical health, and

30

vice versa. The state of our mental health impacts and influences our human relationships, and vice versa.

The scripture references inside the circle point us to some of the specific biblical teachings on what it means to be a healthy person in each area of our total being.

Personal Reflection
~~~~~~~~~~~~~~

Read these scriptures and record your personal thoughts as you reflect on your own state of health and well-being.

Health of one's soul or spirit: John 3:3-5; Proverbs 3:5-8.

Health of the mind and the emotions: Romans 12:1-2; Philippians 4:8.

Health of the body: 1 Corinthians 6:19-20; Philippians 1:20.

Health in human relationships: Matthew 22:39; Colossians 3:12-14.

More insights on wholeness from scripture: As a young man Jesus grew four ways.

> **Luke 2:52, RSV**
> *Jesus increased in wisdom [mind] and in stature [body], and in favor [in favorable relationships] with God and man [with family and neighbors].*

Here is a beautiful benediction for completeness and holiness in every area of our lives.

> **1 Thessalonians 5:23, RSV**
> *May the God of peace himself sanctify you wholly; and may your spirit and soul and body be kept sound [complete] and blameless at the coming of our Lord Jesus Christ.*

Here is another way to visualize human beings wholistically. Again, the circle represents one person. However, because we are basically spiritual beings, made in the image of God (Genesis 1:26-27), this illustration places one's spiritual nature in the center of one's being. The double-pointed arrows depict interaction among one's mind, body, and social relationships.

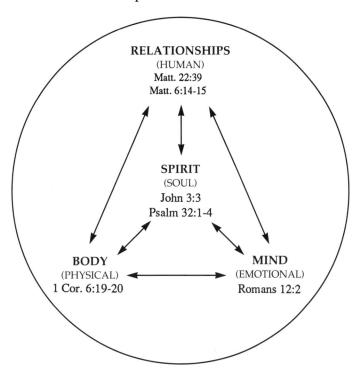

Taking each of the four areas illustrated in the two wholistic concepts, consider the interconnectedness among the parts that often impact the whole person.

1. *Spirit*. Psalm 32:1-4 describes how lack of spiritual health can influence the body and the mind. The psalmist admits that unconfessed sin and heavy guilt resulted in physical problems, insomnia, depression, and low energy levels.

2. *Body*. An unhealthy body can influence one's mind, spirit, and relationships with others. Anyone who has experienced a prolonged physical illness or unrelenting pain can relate to this. Likewise, many who have had surgery know about mental depression in the post-operative stages.

33

3. *Mind*. Negative emotions and attitudes can add stress to our lives that opens the door for disharmony and imbalance physically, spiritually, and in human relationships. Some of these mental states would include resentment, revenge, anger, lack of forgiveness, hate, jealousy, ungratefulness, constant complaining, and criticism.

4. *Relationships*. Broken relationships frequently cause physical and mental anguish. People who make the following comments are usually saying it like it is:

   "She makes me sick to my stomach."

   "That man gives me a pain in the neck."

   "I can't stand to be in the same room with that family."

Personal Reflection
~~~~~~~~~~~~~

Think about your own life experiences as they relate to the wholistic concept of human nature. List some interconnectedness you have known among your body, mind, spirit, and relationships. What other personal illnesses affected and impacted more than one area of your life? Be specific.

Recall a time in your life when you knew what it meant to have balance and to be in harmony with your body, mind, spirit, and relationships. List some factors that influenced that state of good health.

Now take some unhurried moments to write your personal definition of health and wholeness. Be brief—only a sentence or two. Do not look at the following definitions until you have written yours.

Compare your definition to these three:

Albert E. Day
Health is a combination of harmonious relationships, spiritual vitality, psychological maturity, and physical wellness.[7]

Tilda Norberg and Robert D. Webber
Christian healing is a process that involves the totality of our being—body, mind, emotion, spirit, and our social context—and that directs us towards becoming the person God is calling us to be at every stage of our living and our

dying. Whenever we are truly open to God, some kind of healing takes place, because God yearns to bring us to wholeness. Through prayer and the laying on of hands, . . . Jesus meets us in our brokenness and pain and there loves, transforms, forgives, redeems, resurrects, and heals. Jesus does this in God's way, in God's time, and according to God's loving purpose for each person.

Because the Holy Spirit is continually at work in each of us, pushing us toward wholeness, the process of healing is like removing sticks and leaves from a stream until the water runs clear. If we simply get out of the way of the Lord's work in us, we can trust that we are being led to the particular kind of wholeness God wills for us.[8]

Norman Young
We need to be clear about what wholeness, what being fully alive in that sense, is. It does not necessarily mean being released from illness, suffering, weakness or trouble, circumstances often beyond our control. Wholeness means living creatively within our limitations. Not wasting our days in envy at the capacities and capabilities of others; not despairing at the loss of youth and vigour or at the lack of maturity and experience; not giving up when our best efforts produce far less than we had hoped; not torturing ourselves with guilt when having to settle for the lesser of two evils. For to be fully alive . . . is to be whole, fully alive here and now, as things are, not yet in the fulness of God's kingdom which remains in the future. In the meantime we are called to live the life of faith in a world that is still far less than it ought to be, far short of what God intends.[9]

Taking our cue from Jesus, our goal in the church is to develop and maintain "whole-person ministry." We base Christian healing ministry on a wholistic understanding of human nature versus a compartmentalized view. As stated earlier, because Jesus loved the whole person, his goal was to help each person become whole.

36

In summary, the threefold purpose of the healing and wholeness ministry of the church is this:

1. To help one another experience spiritual union with God through Jesus Christ. This healing is the greatest of all. We sometimes call this healing conversion, being born again, regeneration, or spiritual rebirth and renewal.

2. To help one another maintain a harmonious balance in each human being's total system (body, mind, spirit, relationships) day after day, week after week.

3. To help one another restore or repair the total system (body, mind, spirit, relationships) when imbalance, disease, or lack of harmony are evident. We intentionally use all of the therapies that God provides for abundant life, including spiritual, medical, and psychological resources.

Whole-person ministry attempts to treat each person as a unity of body, mind, and spirit. It recognizes the close connection between a person's sense of well-being and self-esteem to one's overall health. It assumes that health is a composite result of emotions and spiritual focus, as well as physical conditions. In practical terms, whole-person ministry approaches each person's illness as multidimensional, particularly dealing with the emotional and spiritual factors that may have contributed to an unbalanced condition.

How is your church doing in whole-person ministry?

Group Reflection/Discussion Guide

Chapter Two: A Wholistic Understanding of Health

~~~~~~~~~~~~~~~~~~~~~~~~~~~~~~~~~~~~~~~

1. Do a Bible study/word study. Matthew 9:20-22 offers an example of the richness of the Greek word *sozo*. (See pages 28–29.) Invite group members to read this passage from a variety of English translations. (Alert the group to this assignment during the prior meeting.) Then discuss the implications of the words *health*, *wholeness*, and *salvation*'s having a common root meaning.

2. Understand human nature wholistically.

   ~ Look at the two graphic illustrations of wholistic human nature (pages 30 and 33). Raise questions and consider comments.

   ~ Invite group members to share personal stories from their life's experiences that demonstrate the interconnectedness of body-mind-spirit relationships (pages 34–35).

3. Define health and wholeness.

   ~ Invite group members to share their personal definitions of health and wholeness (page 35).

   ~ Discuss personal reactions to the definitions of Albert E. Day, Tilda Norberg and Robert D. Webber, and Norman Young (pages 35–36).

4. Take a realistic look at your local church. Invite someone in the group to read aloud the threefold purpose of the healing and wholeness ministry of the church (page 37). Then discuss this question: How well is your church ministering to the whole person?

5. Close by asking group members to join you in praying Albert Day's prayer (page 25).

Chapter Three

Five Kinds of Health

~~~~~~

"IF I AM NOT PHYSICALLY ILL, I do not need the healing ministry." Many people in our churches today who think that healing ministry only deals with physical afflictions and diseases, hold this false notion. However, when we look at Jesus as our model and teacher, we see him dealing with many different forms of illness and unhealthiness. Jesus met people and helped people individually at the point of their personal need in their lifelong journey toward wholeness. Sometimes that personal need was spiritual, physical, emotional, or in relation to other people.

Let us take a closer look at five kinds of health, or five categories of healing ministry.

1. Spiritual Health

Dealing with one's relationship with God is first and primary. Paul Tournier, the famous Swiss physician, believed that a spiritual unrest underlies almost every chronic and acute illness. When this unrest reaches great enough proportions, it throws the body's immune system out of balance. Another medical doctor has stated that twenty-five percent of his patients could be cured by medical means alone, but that seventy-five percent needed the best medical care and the best spiritual care combined. Under the heading of *Spiritual Health* consider the following:

~ *One's personal relationship to God through Jesus Christ.* (See John 3:1-21; 2 Corinthians 5:17-19; Ephesians 2:1-10.) Evangelism and healing are related intricately. Introducing someone to Christ or making a personal commitment to Christ are the first steps toward the greatest healing of all. This process goes by many names: spiritual rebirth, reconciliation with God, being born again, living a Christ-oriented life versus a self-oriented life.

> **George E. Parkinson**
> *The basic purpose of Spiritual Healing is to deepen one's relationship with the living Christ.*[10]

~ *Sin, guilt, and forgiveness.* (See Psalm 103:8-12; Romans 5:8-11.) A Christian psychiatrist, speaking to a large group of pastors and priests said, "I wish people would stop confessing their sins in my office. I cannot forgive sin; only God can deal effectively with sin and guilt. I plead with all Christian ministers to offer the forgiveness and love of God in your churches so that people can be truly released from their sin and guilt."

Yes, God is more ready to forgive than we are to confess. Forgiveness of sin and release from guilt are crucial in the healing process. For further discussion on forgiveness see "Healthy Relationships" (Chapter 3, page 51) and question 11 "How significant is forgiveness in healing ministry?" (Chapter 7, page 116).

~ *The reality of evil.* (See Matthew 6:9-15; Ephesians 1:15-23; 6:10-17; 1 Peter 5:8.) Jesus knew exactly what he was doing when he taught his disciples to pray in his model prayer: "Deliver us from evil" (Matthew 6:13, RSV). He knew that those who declare themselves to be children of God would face unrelenting attack from the forces of evil. However, protection and deliverance from evil are available to all Christians in the name and power that is above all others, the Lord Jesus Christ.

For further discussion on the reality of evil see question 10 "What about exorcism and deliverance in healing ministry?" (Chapter 7, page 113).

Personal Reflection
~~~~~~~~~~~~~

On a scale of 1 to 10 (10 being excellent), rate

~ your overall spiritual health today _____

~ your personal relationship with God _____

~ the way you handle sin, guilt, forgiveness _____

~ the way you deal with the reality of evil _____

Ponder each scripture reference in the section on "Spiritual Health." Allow the Holy Spirit to communicate with your spirit as you open yourself to maximum spiritual health and abundant life in Christ (John 10:10).

2. Physical Health

When we apply prayer therapy to physical illnesses, we may experience one of three possibilities:

~ Instant cure, total remission, or complete healing may occur but are rare. They cannot be predicted or programmed. Instant healing is often called "miraculous" because it happens so fast and without rational or scientific explanation. The only appropriate response to a miracle is to give God the glory.

~ Gradual improvement is the most common experience with prayer. Just as getting sick is a process, so getting well is usually a process. Persons sometimes compare prayers for improved physical health to fast forwarding a videotape. Prayer therapy tends to shorten the healing timetable by speeding up the healing process.

When someone is receptive to prayer therapy, it is not helpful to ask the hard question: "Are you healed?" Rather, gently inquire

"Are you feeling better?"
"Do you notice any improvements?"
"Are you being helped in any way?"
"Any insights into what is going on in your life?"

~ When we see no apparent or obvious improvement in the physical condition, God is faithful and gives us strength and grace to keep on keeping on, to cope, to live with the situation. Why some are healed physically and others are not remains a mystery. However, God's graciousness is operative in many areas of our lives. Those who are committed to the healing ministry of Christ know there are no total failures. When the body is unable to respond to healing, God brings blessings and benefits in other ways.

Immerse yourself in this powerful testimony of Robert Standhardt, a quadriplegic person who, because of a birth injury, uses a walker or a wheelchair wherever he goes.

The greatest disabling conditions that persons face are often not the external physical problems but the ones inside, in the mind and the heart. As a person with an obvious physical handicap, I have seen people cross to the other side of the street rather than meet me, sit in front of me and behind me, and talk all around me in church, and otherwise treat me as if I were unfeeling.

44

Then there are other times (not often enough) when someone will look me in the eye (though they may have to kneel to do this), talk with *me rather than* to *me, sit beside me, and not be afraid to take my hand and communicate that the person accepts and affirms me simply as a person. This is the touch that makes me whole inside, that breathes the Spirit into me. When we touch each other in such love and respect, wholeness comes as Christ's touch becomes our own.* [11]

Even though Robert Standhardt is physically challenged, he is an effective Christian minister and quite whole mentally and spiritually.

Personal Reflection

~~~~~~~~~~~~~

Think about those times when you, your family, or friends prayed for improved physical health. Recall and list some specific circumstances and results.

~ Instant cure, total remission, complete healing:

~ Gradual improvement:

45

~ Grace and strength to cope:

Further thoughts or insights you may want to record:

3. Mental and Emotional Health

One day, while in Jersualem, Jesus came across a group of homeless street people who were sick and disabled. They were living near a pool of water called Bethzatha. According to John 5:1-15, Jesus singled out one man who had been paralyzed for thirty-eight years. Notice the very first words Jesus spoke to the man: "Do you want to be made well?"

Before Jesus could improve the man's physical condition, he had to deal with his state of mind. Perhaps Jesus was attempting to discover the answers to these pertinent issues:

~ What was this man's attitude toward his illness?

~ Had he resigned himself to accepting his unhealthiness as a lifelong situation?

~ Had he actually given up hope of being helped?

Unless we truly want to get well, have an authentic desire to co-operate with God in the healing process, and are open-minded; medical, psychological, and spiritual therapies have limited effectiveness.

Jesus knew that the mind powerfully influences the body. Perhaps the most practical help that Jesus gave everyone he met was hope, along with encouragement. When you have hope and encouragement you can handle just about anything.

Personal Reflection

~~~~~~~~~~~~~~

Read John 5:1-15. Try to put yourself in the situation of the man who was ill for thirty-eight years. Imagine you are that man. Describe your feelings:

~   Before Jesus came along that day:

~   When Jesus asked you, "Do you want to be made well?"

~ At the very moment when Jesus said to you, "Stand up, take your mat and walk."

~ At the moment you walked for the first time in thirty-eight years.

~ When the authorities said to you, "It is the sabbath. It is not lawful for you to carry your mat."

~ When you and Jesus met later that day in the temple and he said to you, "See, you have been made well! Do not sin any more, so that nothing worse happens to you."

Perhaps you know someone who is discouraged totally. Could you be an encourager and a hope-giver to that person? Perhaps you have been living in a "paralyzed" situation for a long time. If so, intentionally invite the compassionate, caring Christ to enter your personal circumstances. Receive his health, wholeness, and salvation.

Dr. E. Stanley Jones, a great Christian leader of a generation ago, was very aware of the mind's effect on the body. In his book, *Christian Maturity*, Dr. Jones makes these strong statements that medical and psychological research are affirming now :

> *We must give up the notion that we can harbor fears, resentments, self-centeredness, and guilts and that nothing will happen to us physically. . . .*
>
> *We must give up the notion that God will pass a miracle over us and heal us without our co-operating with Him in giving up thinking and emotions which produce disease. . . .*
>
> *We must renounce the attitude that we can skip the healing of spirit and take the healing of the body.*[12]

In Romans 12:1-2, St. Paul writes boldly of the necessity for Christians to "be transformed by the renewing of your minds." Through the healing community called the church, God offers us many ways to renew our minds so that we will not be conformed to the world. Some of the spiritual therapies for mind renewal are these: weekly Christian worship, daily prayer, private and group Bible study, regular Holy Communion, devotional reading of the Christian classics, companionship with other Christians, fasting, Christian music, solitude, silence, meditation, and contemplation.

Personal Reflection
~~~~~~~~~~~~~

Some people do little to renew their minds each day. For many the last mind-input before going to bed at night is the late TV newscast and the first mind-input of the day is the early morning TV newscast. In what ways do you try to deal with all of the "bad news" your mind receives each day?

Review the spiritual therapies listed above for mind renewal.

~   List some that you currently practice.

~ List some that you do not practice but could.

Another helpful therapy for mental and emotional health is that of "inner healing" or "the healing of memories." Most of us have memories of people and events that cause us great pain and deep hurt. The therapy of inner healing invites the presence of the healing Christ to go back to those painful moments in our past, to heal the hurt, and to bring release from bondage to those negative memories. Many excellent books are available on the theology and practical helpfulness of inner healing.[13]

The writer of Hebrews gives the most concise statement of the spiritual truth related to the therapy of inner healing:

> ***Hebrews 13:8***
> *Jesus Christ is the same yesterday and today and forever.*

4. Healthy Relationships

According to Jesus, the kingdom of God is a kingdom of right relationships. When he was asked to name the greatest commandment, this was Jesus' response:

> ***Matthew 22:37-39***
> *"You shall love the Lord your God with all your heart, and with all your soul, and with all your mind." This is the greatest and first commandment. And a second is like it: "You shall love your neighbor as yourself."*

Personal Reflection

~~~~~~~~~~~~~

Ask yourself a tough question: How healthy are my relationships with the people that Jesus calls neighbor? On a scale of 1 to 10 (10 being excellent) rate your relationship health today with

~ your family _____

~ your friends _____

~ your colleagues at work _____

~ your church pastor _____

~ your church lay leader _____

~ church members _____

~ the people you meet when you go shopping _____
    when you go driving _____
    when you go walking _____
    when you go to a restaurant _____

Jesus says we are supposed to love these "neighbors" as much as we love ourselves.

On a scale of 1 to 10, how much do I love myself today? _____

Jesus knew that we would find it difficult to maintain loving, caring relationships. So he frequently discussed the need for forgiveness. Although forgiveness is the most effective therapy in healing broken relationships, it is also very hard to do day in and day out. We constantly call on the grace and help of Christ.

Closely related to forgiveness is the therapy of inner healing. Many persons have experienced traumatic abuse and damaged emotions in their past. As part of the forgiveness process, painful memories and woundedness need to be healed. This takes time and the skill of a gentle, compassionate Christian therapist.

Forgiveness truly is a key to good health, benefiting the forgiver as much or even more than the one being forgiven.

52

Having learned to let go of unhealthy stress brought on by resentment, bitterness, and anger, forgiving people are happier people. Remember: Forgiveness takes time; it is a process not an event.

For further discussion on forgiveness, see question 11 "How significant is forgiveness in healing ministry?" (Chapter Seven, page 116).

Personal Reflection
~~~~~~~~~~~~~

A Private Devotional Exercise on Forgiveness
Mary Lou Wagner

In the quiet of your room or your favorite devotional spot, take some unhurried time to ponder these thoughts:

When someone hurts me or fails to meet my expectations, am I able to forgive him or her immediately without harboring a grudge and without frequently rehearsing my grievance in my mind?

If the answer is no, in what ways does my resentment work itself out in my life and in my attitude toward that person? How do I feel about that person? How do I feel about myself? (Do not rush.)

Next, make a list of persons you cannot stand to be around,

~ who have been unkind to you,

~ who go out of their way to hurt you,

~ who insist on their own way,

~ who do not listen to you,

~ who constantly try to change you,

~ who put you down.

Then check out how you feel about yourself.

~ In what areas do you need to forgive yourself?

What about your relationship with God?

~ In what ways are you upset or angry with God?

~ In what ways do you feel God has let you down?

Ask God, in your own sincere way, to forgive you and to cleanse you of all resentment and hurt feelings. As the love begins to flow from God to you and from you to God, ask God to fill you with peace and joy.

Return to your list of persons, lifting up each one by name into the light and love of the healing, forgiving Christ. Intentionally forgive each one, just as God through Christ forgives you. (Take your time.)

Offer your personal prayer of thanksgiving. Amen.[14]

5. Ultimate Health in the Resurrection Following the Death of the Body

Christians understand death of the physical body as a process one goes through in order to experience the ultimate healing and wholeness in the resurrection of Jesus Christ. Statement 10 in the True/False Quiz is *false*. Death does not heal; rather, death is a transition to more life, to perfect wholeness, to ultimate health, to complete harmony with God.

Christians are an Easter People who claim and who live by all of Jesus' promises. Jesus himself reminds us of the ultimate promise, and the writer of the Gospel of John recalls for us the gift that God offers.

> *John 11:25-26*
> *I am the resurrection and the life. Those who believe*
> *in me, even though they die, will live, and everyone*
> *who lives and believes in me will never die.*

Tommy Tyson
The basis of healing [is] the Incarnation, Crucifixion, and Resurrection. Otherwise, healing is simply a temporary alleviation of a symptom. That's all. But in the light of the resurrection and ascension, healing is a sneak preview of the ultimate. We're going to be changing to His likeness, have a body like unto His own glorious body. Our eyes won't need glasses; our knees won't have arthritis; our tongues won't gossip. We are going to have a resurrected body like unto His own.

That's the glorious foundation for the healing ministry for the Church.[15]

Even though Christians regularly affirm belief in "the resurrection of the body, and the life everlasting," many continue to prize physical health as the very essence of life. Granted, God intends for each of us to enjoy maximum physical well-being. However, the Christian has a broader perspective.

Personal Reflection
~~~~~~~~~~~~

Ponder these two statements:

~ **All human beings are terminal, physically speaking.**

Our creator did not design the human body to last forever. Physical death is an inescapable reality for each of us. What is the maximum number of years a person might expect to live, given no accidents, no disease, proper balance of caloric intake and physical exercise? Some studies in gerontology suggest 120 years could be the maximum human age. It is interesting to note a verse in Genesis.

Genesis 6:3
Then the LORD said, "My spirit shall not abide in mortals forever, for they are flesh; their days shall be one hundred twenty years."

Although someone might live to be 120, like an automobile with 120,000 miles there comes a point when the aging vehicle cannot go another inch.

Have you accepted your own physical mortality? If not, why not?

If you have, how does this acceptance influence your attitude and outlook on life?

~   **All physical healing is temporary.**

Even a miraculous, dramatic healing does not guarantee permanent health. Because of the aging process, it is only a matter of time before another malfunction or breakdown of the physical system occurs.

One of the saints used to pray:

O Lord, each day I am growing older and some day I shall be old.

Am I accepting my humanness, knowing that I will not need my physical body in the resurrection? Am I learning to live creatively within my limitations? You may want to record your thoughts.

A minister in the British Methodist Church, who was preaching on the topic, "When Healing Does Not Happen," shared a therapeutic word for all of us.

Reginald Mallett
Sometimes the human body does not respond to any kind of therapy. However, when the container in which we live is hopelessly flawed, the contents can be wonderfully whole.[16]

Let us affirm each day, with sincere thanksgiving, the tension all Christians experience between living with less than complete wholeness and looking forward to the ultimate healing in the resurrection.

1 Corinthians 15:50, 54, 57
Flesh and blood cannot inherit the kingdom of God, nor does the perishable inherit the imperishable. . . .When this perishable body puts on imperishability, and this mortal body

puts on immortality, then the saying that is written will be fulfilled: "Death has been swallowed up in victory." . . . Thanks be to God, who gives us the victory through our Lord Jesus Christ.

Personal Reflection

~~~~~~~~~~~~~

Five kinds of health: spiritual, physical, mental/emotional, relationships, and ultimate health in the resurrection. Record your feelings and thoughts as you apply all five to your personal life and situation.

Group Reflection/Discussion Guide

Chapter Three: Five Kinds of Health

~~~~~~~~~~~~~~~~~~~~~~~~~

1. Invite group members to share and discuss any ideas, thoughts, feelings they had while reading this chapter. Consider the five kinds of health: spiritual, physical, mental/emotional, relationships, and ultimate health in the resurrection.

2. Discuss this statement: "When you have hope and encouragement, you can handle just about anything" (page 47). Name some persons who have given you hope and encouragement:

   Name some persons you know who seem to have very little hope and are very discouraged. Perhaps you could be an encourager and hope-giver:

3. Read 1 Corinthians 15:35-58. Be sure each person has a Bible. Read this passage aloud, followed by unhurried silence for personal reflection. Invite the group to discuss this passage in relation to the following statement: "Death is a transition to . . . ultimate health" (page 54).

4. Invite the group to enter into this guided meditation, remembering that forgiveness is a process, not an event. Prepare for an uninterrupted, unhurried time of prayer. Get as comfortable as possible, breathing deeply, relaxing your mind and body, being open and receptive to the Holy Spirit. Then ask someone to pray the following prayer aloud:

We adore you, O Christ, we praise you, O Christ, because through your holy cross you have redeemed the world and saved each of us from his or her sins. Through your holy cross you have forgiven us and loved us even before we knew what forgiveness and love were all about. (pause)

Right now, O Christ, each one of us comes to you seeking help in being a forgiving person. (pause)

Some of us are having difficulty forgiving. We need your strength and a willingness to be willing to forgive. Help each of us overcome stubbornness and pride that cripple us in so many ways. (pause)

And now, O Christ, in a conscious, deliberate act of our will, we want to forgive everyone who has anything against any of us.

Some of us need to forgive our parents. (pause)

Some of us need to forgive our children. (pause)

Some of us need to forgive God, our heavenly Father. (pause)

Some of us need to forgive ourselves. (pause)

Some of us need to forgive someone who died before we were reconciled. (pause)

Lord, hear our prayers as we pray specifically by name.

Lord, I forgive ____(name)____. (Pause for personal prayers of forgiveness in silence.)

Lord, we now turn over to you, ourselves and all those persons we have named in forgiveness. As you direct any of us to take tangible action, give us the will to follow through (perhaps a phone call, a personal letter, an apology, or restitution).

60

Gracious, merciful Lord, help each one of us know the joy of forgiveness; the joy of burdens taken away; the joy of new life in Christ; the joy of health and wholeness in body, mind, spirit, and in all relationships. In the name of the Father, the Son, and the Holy Spirit we pray and dedicate ourselves. Amen.[17]

Chapter Four

The Christian Life as a Journey toward Wholeness

~~~~~~

*T*WELVE MINISTERS AND THEOLOGIANS OF ALL FAITHS *and twelve psychiatrists of all faiths had convened for a two-day, off-the-record seminar on the one-word theme of* healing. *The chairman, a psychiatrist, opened the seminar with [these] question[s]: "We are all healers, whether we are ministers or doctors. Why are we in this business? What is our motivation?" There followed only ten minutes of intense discussion, and they all agreed, doctors and ministers, Catholics, Jews, and Protestants. "For our own healing," they said.*

This is an interesting word, healing, *with its meaning "to make whole." The example above suggests that one really never makes it. It is always something sought. Perhaps, as with the minister and the doctor, the servant-leader might also acknowledge that his [or her] own healing is his [or her] motivation. There is something subtle communicated to one who is being served and led if, implicit in the compact between the servant-leader and led, is the understanding that the search for wholeness is something they share.*[18]

The search for wholeness and health is the primary quest of all human beings (healthiness and completeness of body, mind, spirit, and relationships). Persons often describe this common quest as a faith journey or as a spiritual journey. Christians sometimes refer to themselves as pilgrims on a journey. John Wesley liked the metaphor of journeying and frequently mentioned it in his writings.

Once when he was accosted by an overbearing, drunken traveler who barraged him with questions about his destination, Wesley reminded him that all of humanity is on a longer journey, traveling toward eternity.

For Wesley, the Christian sense of believing meant walking in the way of eternity. "The way" for Wesley meant the path of salvation. By salvation he meant not simply a blessing that lies on the other side of death, in the "other world." Salvation was not something at a distance. Nor was it a momentary event, disconnected from other life experiences. With the term *salvation*, Wesley wanted to designate the entire redemptive work of God—from the first dawning of grace in a person's life to the final consummation and ultimate wholeness and healing in the resurrection.

Yes, salvation is a way of being and living in the world, a way Wesley characterized best as "love." His elevation of love did not lessen the significance of faith. After his 1738 Aldersgate experience of deep, personal assurance that Christ had indeed died for his sins, loved him, and given himself fully for him, Wesley was certain that love itself was impossible except as a fruit of faith. Wesley believed that faith was the only condition of the Christian's acceptance and justification by God, and he agreed that faith was a gift of God's amazing grace.

Furthermore, Wesley held that one's love or lack of love toward God, neighbor, and self had a direct bearing on one's health and wholeness. Therefore, he could speak of love as the medicine of life, the remedy for the evils of a disordered world and all the miseries and vices of men and women. Yet Wesley also emphasized that even the soul perfected by love often had to endure the ills of a shattered body.

John Wesley's high appreciation of love as the more excellent way, reminds us of the Apostle Paul's "love chapter," 1 Corinthians 13. Yet neither Paul nor Wesley had an ideal, easy, ever-ascending, spiritual journey. Both men experienced frequent setbacks, untold disappointments, as well as significant advances along their spiritual journeys.

God gives each of us a personal spiritual history uniquely different from the individual journeys of other human beings. Have you discovered that God is able to use all of your experiences (the good ones as well as the not-so-good ones) in amazing ways when you give God permission to do so, when you go with the flow of God's spirit from day to day? Record some of your insights from those experiences below.

Have you experienced the truth of these thoughts recorded by Paul?

Romans 8:28
We know that all things work together for good for those who love God, who are called according to his purpose.

Paul did not write that God causes all things. He writes that God's gracious, guiding, empowering Holy Spirit can work beneficially in all circumstances and situations.

When bad things happen to good people, the helpful question is not "Why did this happen to me"; rather, "Now that this has happened, what might be my next step, knowing that I can count on God's help?"

Personal Reflection

~~~~~~~~~~~~~~

Reflect unhurriedly on Romans 8:28. List some not-so-good personal experiences that are part of your past.

	WHAT HAPPENED?	YOUR RESPONSE THEN	OUTCOME NOW
10 YEARS			
5 YEARS			
1 YEAR			

Write down any new thoughts you may have at this moment:

66

Each of us has a uniquely personal spiritual history. Fold a blank piece of paper lengthwise. Open the paper. Write the year you were born at the far left of the center line. Write the current year at the far right of the center line.

Then along your timeline, write dates and events, names of family members, friends and other persons who played a positive role in your faith development. Perhaps you can name some helpful books, movies, plays, or music. What may have seemed like insignificant decisions, unimportant moments, unspectacular situations may reveal God's gracious movements in your life. List all of these along your timeline. Do not hurry.

You may want to do this reflective exercise once each year—on your birthday or on New Year's Day. Meditate with thanksgiving on God's amazing grace moments in your last 365 days. These grace moments will remind you again and again that you are God's child; and like a loving, caring, compassionate parent, God never abandons you. This recall of God's helpfulness in your past can be a powerful affirmation of God's presence now and in your future. Thanks be to God!

Yes, the quest for wholeness and health is a journey everyone shares. The Christian finds this trek constantly punctuated with tensions of many sorts. Although we rightfully claim Christ's promise of abundant life, we also live in a world that holds values contrary to the gospel.

In her book *Growing Strong at Broken Places*, Paula Ripple quotes a wise woman potter:

Both my hands shaped this pot. And, the place where it actually forms is a place of tension between the pressure applied from the outside and the pressure of the hand on the inside. That's the way my life has been. Sadness and death and misfortune and the love of friends and all the things that happened to me that I didn't even choose. All of that influenced my life. But, there are things I believe in about myself, my faith in God and the love of some friends that worked on the insides of me. My life, like this pot, is the result of what happened on the outside and what was going on inside of me. Life, like this pot, comes to be in places of tension. Life comes to be when we learn how to avoid looking for answers and finally learn how to ask the questions that will bring us to life.[19]

The writer goes on to comment that all of us tend to want to live tension free. But, like the woman potter, she feels that this tension is God's gift to us, a gift that sometimes will not permit us to escape its presence. She believes that that kind of upsetting tension activates our creative energies. In responding to this gnawing discomfort, we have the possibility of giving shape to dreams that are at once faithful to who we are and to who we can become. Consider the benefits of creatively using unavoidable stress.

James Fenhagen

The Christian journey is a life lived from inside out, a life in which the things we experience within—dreams, memories, images, and symbols, and the presence of [God] whom we encounter in the deep silence—are in constant tension and dialogue with all that we experience without: people, events, joys, sorrows, and the presence of [God] whom we encounter in others. Thomas Merton repeats a suggestion of Douglas Steere that the absence of this tension might well produce the most pervasive form of violence present in contemporary society. "To allow one's self to be carried away by a multitude of conflicting concerns," Merton writes, "to surrender to too many demands, to commit one's self to too many projects, to want to help everyone in everything is to succumb to violence. Frenzy destroys our inner capacity for peace. It destroys the fruitfulness of our work, because it kills the root of inner wisdom which makes work fruitful.

"One of the most critical tasks of the local church is to enable people to become 'journeyers' rather than 'wanderers.' This suggests that the leadership of a congregation needs to be serious about their own journeys, to the point where they are willing to share their

experience with others, not as those who have arrived but
as fellow journeyers able to receive as well as to give."[20]

As you continue to reflect on your personal spiritual journey ponder these two questions:

1. What area of my life still needs the healing and wholeness of Jesus Christ?

2. Having recalled and remembered God's gracious help in my past, where do I see God leading me next?

Pray this prayer of affirmation and hope:

Gracious and Loving God,
truly like a good shepherd you know me by name.
Gently you lead me day after day after day.
Even though I do not know what the future holds,
I do know that you are in my future.
Therefore, I can live fully and without fear in the present
because your Holy Spirit is with me, loving me, guiding me,
empowering me, and healing me through Jesus Christ who
is the same yesterday, today, and forever. Amen!

Group Reflection/Discussion Guide

*Chapter Four: The Christian Life as a
Journey toward Wholeness*

~~~~~~~~~~~~~~~~~~~

1. Read Romans 8:28 aloud to the group, followed by two minutes of silence.

    ~ Invite those who are willing to share how the spiritual principles in Romans 8:28 have worked out in some of their personal situations.

    ~ Discuss the statement: "When bad things happen to good people, the helpful question is not 'Why did this happen to me'; rather, 'Now that this has happened, what might be my next step, knowing that I can count on God's help?'" (page 65).

2. Share spiritual journeys. The reading and exercises asked each person to reflect on his or her unique spiritual history. (See page 67, which outlines this exercise.) Distribute paper and pencils to those who may not have done this exercise. Allow five minutes for the group members to work silently on their spiritual journeys. Those who already did the exercise can continue to reflect and write.

    Invite the group members to pair off with someone they do not know well and share some things from their individual journeys with each other. Allow six minutes, giving each person three minutes to share. Then call the group together, inviting responses to these questions:

~ What experiences of God in your life did you and your partner have in common? in contrast?

~ Has this reflecting on your past revealed an insight or a new learning?

3. Ask someone to read the quotations by Paula Ripple and James Fenhagen (pages 67–69) aloud if time permits. Invite comments and discussion.

4. Reflect silently on these two questions:

~ What area of my life still needs the healing and wholeness of Jesus Christ?

~ Having recalled and remembered God's gracious help in my past, where do I see God leading me next?

Then pray in unison the prayer of affirmation and hope (page 69).

Chapter Five

Prayer and Healing

~~~~~~

WELL-MEANING PEOPLE OFTEN SAY, "We've done everything we can think to do. Now, all we can do is pray." What a sad commentary on prayer! Many Christians understand prayer as a last resort rather than as a primary resource in combating illnesses and in coping with personal problems.

Prayer for healing is not human effort to change God's mind. Christ's healing ministry already has revealed that the mind of God is on the side of good health. Prayer for healing is a way to make us more receptive and more willing to receive what God already has prepared for us in Christ and through the Holy Spirit.

Think of prayer as cooperation with God. Think of prayer as giving God permission to move and to act in our lives.

God respects our human freedom. God gave all of us free will to make our own choices in life. In this sense, God patiently waits to offer assistance. Through intentional times of prayer, we give God those grace-filled opportunities.

When we pray for our own healing or the healing of another, we are not in a begging posture; rather, we are intentionally cooperating with God's good will for health, wholeness, and salvation. Because the Apostle Paul understood prayer as cooperation with God and as a way for Christians to give God permission to act in our lives, he wrote the following:

Philippians 4:6-7
Do not worry about anything, but in everything by prayer and supplication with thanksgiving let your requests be made known to God. And the peace of God, which surpasses all understanding, will guard your hearts and your minds in Christ Jesus.

Paul is clear that we should pray "in everything," not in "some things." What about those Christians who have two worry lists—one they take to God in prayer and one they fret and stew about but do not pray about. Some of us think that God is too big and too busy to care about everything we are facing, such as minor irritations in life: a sick pet, a pesky headache, an upset stomach, a parking place when shopping time is short, a sprained ankle, or being able to sleep at night.

Is there a word of guidance from Paul's instruction to pray "in everything"? The Quaker Elton Trueblood once said in a classroom lecture: "Whatever is worth worrying about is worth praying about."

Personal Reflection
~~~~~~~~~~~~~

What things are you currently worrying about and praying about?

74

What things concern you—perhaps even worry you—but you are not praying about them?

1 Peter 5:7
Cast all your anxiety on him, because he cares for you.

By sharing our worries and anxieties with God who cares deeply for each of us, we are allowing the Holy Spirit to bring fresh options and solutions to seemingly impossible situations.

Consider the question: Are there some things God either cannot or will not do until people pray? Before dismissing this possibility, think of the many sermons we have heard that have told us that we are God's hands, feet, and agents in the world. Through God's people, God accomplishes acts of mercy, deeds of kindness, expressions of love, and deliberate peacemaking activities in a fragmented and fractured world.

Maxie Dunnam
What if there are some things God either cannot or will not do until people pray? . . . Why is it such a long leap in our minds to think that God is as dependent upon our praying as he is upon our acting?[21]

The Old Testament challenges us with a strong statement to pray first and then to experience God's promises.

2 Chronicles 7:14
If my people who are called by my name humble themselves, pray, seek my face, and turn from their wicked ways, then I will hear from heaven, and will forgive their sin and heal their land.

John Bunyan
You can do no more than pray, after you have prayed, but you cannot do more than pray until you have prayed.[22]

The last resort? No! Prayer is our God-given primary therapy for hope, help, and healing in all of life's situations and possibilities. What exactly is prayer?

Personal Reflection
~~~~~~~~~~~~~~

Before examining the relationship between prayer and healing, take a few minutes to reflect on your personal definition of prayer. In a sentence or two complete this statement: For me prayer is

Now compare your idea of prayer to these concepts:

Steve Harper
The real purpose and value of prayer is intimacy with God, not acquisition from God.[23]

James Montgomery
Prayer is the soul's sincere desire, unuttered or expressed.[24]

Frank B. Stanger
Prayer is not over-coming God's reluctance. Prayer is laying hold of God's highest goodness.[25]

76

Ten-year-old boy in Sunday school
Prayer is like accessing God's modem on your computer-based teleconferencing network.

Six-year-old girl in church
Prayer is like using a telephone. Sometimes you talk and sometimes you listen.

Alice L. Pinto
Prayer can be as simple as basking in the sunshine of God's love.[26]

The Book of Revelation records a significant biblical image of prayer.

Revelation 3:20
[Christ says:] *Listen! I am standing at the door, knocking; if you hear my voice and open the door, I will come in to you and eat with you, and you with me.*

Fenelon, a Catholic archbishop of the late seventeenth century, gives us a powerful metaphor for prayer: "The wind of God is always blowing, but you must hoist your sail."

Think of prayer as hoisting your spiritual sail in order to go with the flow of God's Holy Spirit day after day. List some other ways to describe the dynamics of prayer.

Having considered the basics of prayer, let us now look at the relationship between prayer and the process of healing.

Albert E. Day
The purpose of prayer is to open our whole selves to divine intervention; to grant God a welcome; . . . to invite God to

*be to us more than a bare necessity of our very existence;
to give God "the freedom of the city," the key to all that we
are and all that we may become by heavenly action upon
our willingness.*

True prayer is the opening of our minds *to the divine
consciousness. . . .*

True prayer is the opening of our hearts *to the divine
presence by renouncing our petty affections, our juvenile
aversions, our adult passions and resentments, our socially
conditioned fears and frenzies, all of which hamper God's
effort to help and to heal. In true prayer there is always a
housecleaning, an examination of self in the light of Christ,
a "change of heart." . . .*

True prayer is an opening of our wills *to God.*

*True prayer sets God free in a human life. It does not
persuade God to heal. It permits God to do what is necessary for any real healing of disease of the body and mind
and spirit.* [27]

List your personal thoughts and questions related to prayer and
healing:

It is one thing to pray; it is quite another matter to pray believing that prayer makes a difference. To believe that prayer helps in the healing process, one must also believe that the spiritual world is real and that the spiritual dimension in the healing process is to be taken seriously.

Christians believe that the Word of God became flesh and lived among us in the person of Jesus (John 1:1-14). In the Lord's Prayer, we affirm that God communicates with us from the spiritual realm with power to change our lives in the physical world.

Matthew 6:10
Your kingdom come. Your will be done, on earth as it is in heaven.

How seriously do we take the spiritual world? Gordon Dalbey, a minister in the United Church of Christ, discusses some of the fears we may have about the spiritual world.

Because the realm of the spirit is at once powerful, largely unknown and beyond our control, it threatens us. . . . We fear losing faith and losing face if it doesn't "work.". . . Better to stay comfortably ignorant and just go through the motions, praying in eloquent generalities, so you can never tell if your prayer is heard or not.[28]

Years ago, Gordon Dalbey was a Peace Corps volunteer among some very primitive people.

I had a battery-powered tape recorder which amazed and frightened the villagers where I lived. "It's magic!" they exclaimed upon hearing their own voices mimicked by the little "wheel box." Our Western-scientific reaction is, "Tape recording is not magic; it is something we have developed by applying the laws of the universe properly." Yet in the spiritual realm, our Western-scientific mind is patently primitive.[29]

Personal Reflection

~~~~~~~~~~~~~~

How seriously do you take the spiritual world? Reflect on these questions:

~ Do I believe that the spiritual realm is real?

~ Do I take the spiritual dimension in the healing process seriously?

~ Do I pray, believing that prayer makes a positive difference?

Those who do believe the spiritual world is real; those who do take the spiritual dimension in the healing process seriously; those who do pray believing that prayer makes a positive difference, know without doubt that a beneficial relationship between prayer and healing exists.

According to a resource used by the International Prayer Fellowship, increasing numbers of health care professional persons are exploring "the faith factor" in the healing process. Cardiologist Dr. Randy Byrd affirms that prayer is good for the body as well as the soul. He assigned 393 heart patients, each of whom had been admitted to the coronary care unit during a ten-month period, to two groups. The doctor factored the patients' ages and the severity of their disease into the division process.

Dr. Byrd then located persons around the country who agreed to pray once a day for each one of the 192 patients in the experimental group. Each patient in this group had from five to seven people praying for him or her but were not told so by the researchers. The second group, or control group, of 201 patients didn't have individuals praying for them.

Dr. Byrd found that the "prayed-for" patients had significantly fewer instances of complications. Only three required antibiotics, compared to sixteen in the control group. Only six suffered from fluid in the lungs, compared to eighteen in the control group. None of the "prayed-for" patients required artificial respiration, compared to twelve of those in the control group who did.

80

Barbara Von Frogge, a psychology teacher, said that the psychologists agree that a person's thoughts affect the body.

We know that the brain releases chemicals. More than two hundred of these are mood-altering. So what you think, you do produce in your brain chemically.

Taking that medical base, I believe, when you pray, there is a balancing that takes place in the body. You relax. The Holy Spirit has a power of its own that relaxes you and makes you function as God intended.[30]

Personal Reflection
~~~~~~~~~~~~

An Experience in Imaging Prayer
Matthew H. Gates

Part I

It's 7:00 A.M. Monday morning at Boston's Deaconess Hospital. I am preparing myself to walk through the valley of the shadow of open heart surgery. Two nights earlier the surgeon had breezed into the room, briefly identified himself as my surgeon to be, and quickly left saying he would be back to talk with me before the surgery. It was to take place Monday afternoon.

I have long been convinced that we are one being of two parts—body and soul; and that to have wholeness and health, both parts must be ministered to and in harmony. I knew I had a major part to play in this surgery in bringing my spiritual forces to their highest possible level. So I had been actively working at it as I whiled away the hours of waiting.

By the time Dr. Stephen Lahey, grandson of the founder of Boston's famous Lahey Clinic, came into the room that Monday morning, a holy calm had settled over my life. I was completely at ease. Dr. Lahey began to tell me all the positive things about my situation: that I was in the prime group for successful heart bypass surgery, and so on. Then he ran through the list of negative possibilities, the things that could go wrong but were not likely to. He asked me how I felt about it all. I told him I was ready and confident. I used the words *holy calm*, saying that I have a "holy calm" within and that I am free of all anxiety and tension.

I began to tell him about the exercises in spiritual imaging that I had been doing. I pointed to the three or four bags of IVs that were hanging over my head and said that I knew that drop by drop they were preparing my body. I said to him, "I have two other invisible IVs that are also ministering to me. One of those invisible IVs comes from within me, the other from without.

First the one from without. The news of my surgery had gone out via the magic communication of the telephone. Coming back from the north, south, east, and west were the prayers and thoughts of my family, my friends, my former colleagues in ministry. They were being gathered at the feet of God and drop by drop by drop they were feeding into my psyche and my soul, bringing new strength and confidence. I could see that the doctor was listening intently.

The other IV, I said, comes from within myself. It's made up of all the verses, bits of scripture or hymns, the lines from great prayers of the church that had been running through my mind. When I couldn't remember words, I would hum the hymn tune, and the message would get through. Drop by drop by drop, this IV began shaping and strengthening my outlook, my faith, my hope as I focused on the goodness, the love, the caring, the constancy of God. Together, they made me grateful for all that had been and hopeful for all that was to be.

There was a moment of silence. Then Dr. Lahey thanked me for sharing with him. He affirmed his own belief that the attitude of the patient was an integral part of successful surgery. Then he attested to his own faith as a devout mass-going Roman Catholic. Again, there was a moment of silence. He pulled a paper out of his pocket and said that he needed my release to authorize the surgery and said, "We'll make a covenant on your Bible." Taking my Bible from my table he handed it to me along with a pen and said, "I offer my best surgical skills, you bring your sense of holy calm, and we'll both trust God to make this a successful surgery." With that he left. In forty-four years of ministry, never had I experienced such a powerful moment of bonding between doctor and patient. It was truly a holy moment.

Part II

Following the conversation with the doctor, I began to think what I wanted to say to my family. I knew my wife and sons and daughter would be coming to Boston from the Cape to "send me off." They were planning on the schedule of afternoon surgery. Suddenly I learned that the time for the surgery had been moved up, and I was concerned that they might not get here in time for me to talk with them.

The spiritual imaging that I had been doing had shifted. I thought of life as a wonderful gift that is given. It begins in a mysterious moment of time; it will end just as mysteriously. In between, it is like a great river that flows through the land giving to and taking from the good and the ills of its surroundings. Over and over again the old song we used to sing at camp, "Peace I ask of thee, O River, peace, peace, peace," kept running through my mind.

I thought of my body, "fearfully and wonderfully made," and how it exists in a natural environment where its inner parts relate to realities in that natural environment. I had been reading the material, given by the hospital, on the central function of the heart; literally the power center of the body. From ancient times life has been said to focus in the heart. The link between life in the body and the natural environment comes by way of the lungs that naturally breathe in the oxygen that keeps the heart going so that it in turn can give life to all our senses. A reality out there in the environment relates in a mysterious way to each one of our senses. It is a part of the creative gift of life God has given to us.

There are great thoughts and wisdom toward which the mind can reach that expands our lives. To match our sight there is a multitude of colors and faces to be seen. For our hearing, there are the enriching sounds of music, of voice or instrument. To touch a petal of a flower, to feel sand under your feet, a gentle breeze on your skin, to feel another person, brings exhilaration into life. To taste a luscious strawberry, or a sun-ripened tomato, or a thousand other sensations, brings joy to the palate.

Just as there is a natural or physical environment in which we live and move and have our being, so there is a spiritual environment in which we also live and move and have our being that relates with equal reality to an inner sense. We speak of it as the soul. It functions as naturally as the lungs in bringing into our inner being the vitality of the presence of God. How majestic the thought that by a turning of the mind I can be in the direct presence of God—drawing on God's love, power, peace, joy. What a song it puts into my heart. What confidence and strength it brings to life.

The imagery shifted slightly again. Being aware of the thoughts and prayers of my family and friends was like an electric impulse. As more and more prayers were offered, the strength of the impulses increased, setting up a dynamic force in the spiritual environment in which I lived. Just as in the biblical story when healing came with the stirring of the waters, so in this moment I felt the stirring of the Spirit bringing me to calmness, peace, and hope; and I knew that I was being healed.

I was given my preoperative medication and placed on the stretcher to move toward the operating room. Just as I was wheeled into the corridor, Alice and the boys arrived. I asked the nurse for a few more minutes. She found a way to delay a bit, and I shared with my family what I had been thinking and feeling—that I lived by the fact that, as the hymn stated, "Grace hath brought me safe thus far," and I am certain that grace will see me through, that I was in God's keeping. The medicine took its toll, and the beginning of a wonderful "lost day" had started.

Part III

This strange spiritual pilgrimage has a prologue and a sequel. In some mysterious way a most unusual set of coincidences occurred that no one could ever have planned or foreseen.

The day I entered the hospital, the surprised victim of a heart problem, Alice gave me the current issue of *Reader's Digest*, which she had picked up in the hospital news shop. It is not a magazine we usually buy, but she happened to notice its lead story—"The Legend of the Four Chaplains." It was the story of the four chaplains—a Roman Catholic priest, a Jewish rabbi, and two Protestant ministers—who in World War II, when the troopship *Dorchester* was sunk, gave away their own life jackets, linked arms in prayer, and went down with the ship. One of those chaplains was my best friend,

84

and perhaps the human instrument that God used to begin the process of leading me into the ministry.

Being an orphan, I had no male figure in my life. When I was twelve, Clark Poling, then a student at the Yale Divinity School, came to the South Meriden Church as its student pastor. He became my role model. He made it possible for me to attend a week at camp at an interdenominational church camp. In the second summer at the camp, I began to feel that perhaps God might be able to use me in ministry. Our second son is named after Chaplain Clark Poling. How strange that the reminder of Clark and his influence on my life should come back into my life at this crucial moment.

I learned about the next two strange connections the day after surgery. That day the head nurse in the operating room at Deaconess Hospital in Boston just happened to be a young woman who had been a member of our young adult group during my ministry at old St. John's Church in New Rochelle, NY some thirty years ago (St. John's later merged with First Church to become Christ Church, New Rochelle). I had performed the wedding for this young lady and later baptized her first child.

An operating room is essentially an event in anonymity. There is a task to perform and a body to be worked on. Perhaps, except for the surgeon, you have no name. By a strange coincidence, on the way to sign out a supply of blood in preparation for the surgery this nurse happened to note the name on the chart—M. Gates. It evoked the thought, *I once knew a person by that name.* She told me later, "I don't know what moved me to do it, but I went back to take a second look at the chart and family record." She saw my wife's name— Alice—and then she saw the title: Reverend Matthew H. Gates. She said she let out a scream that startled everyone in the operating room. "I know that man," she shouted. "He performed my wedding!"

By still another coincidence, a young medical student was a part of the team of anesthesiologists that day. He heard the scream and said, "Oh, I know him too. He is the minister who married my in-laws to be and who baptized my fiancé. I met him a few years ago." His in-laws to be, of all the couples I have married, are among the most spiritually alive and vital persons that I know of. I have had close contact with them over the years and have rejoiced in their spiritual maturing.

A moment of celebration was going on in that operating room, all unbeknown to me, linking my past with the harsh reality of the present that had brought me here and opening the door to all of the future that lies ahead. I have no explanation of why these wonderful coincidences occurred. Perhaps God understood that I was in a lonely place and sent me friends to keep me company and to help out in the healing ways to which they had been called to serve.[31]

(Note: Successful surgery followed this experience of imaging prayer in the late 1980s. Today Matthew M. Gates is fully recovered.)

The implications are quite clear. Combine the best medical therapies and the best spiritual therapies to give God more to work with in the healing process.

If you or someone you know have had illnesses that responded in positive ways to prayer therapy, list some of the circumstances and details for reflection:

In summarizing this chapter that focuses on the relationship between prayer and healing, Christians affirm that

1. Prayer enables us to cooperate with God in the healing process.
2. Prayer helps remove barriers to the healing process.
3. Prayer often speeds up the healing process.

Group Reflection/Discussion Guide

Chapter Five: Prayer and Healing

~~~~~~~~~~~~~~~~~~~~~~

1. Share Dr. E. Stanley Jones's witness, found in his pamphlet, *How to Pray.* It gives a powerful testimony to the role of prayer in everyday living. Let the group reflect on and discuss his statement:

   If I had one gift, and only one gift, to make to the Christian Church, I would offer the gift of prayer. For everything follows from prayer.

   Prayer tones up the total life. I find by actual experience I am better or worse as I pray more or less. If my prayer life sags, my whole life sags with it; if my prayer life goes up, my life as a whole goes up with it. To fail here is to fail all down the line; to succeed here is to succeed everywhere.

   In the prayer time the battle of the spiritual life is lost or won. Prayer is not an optional subject in the curriculum of living. It is a required subject; it is the *required subject. And there is no graduation into adequate human living without prayer.*[32]

2. Read this comment on healing prayer by Tilda Norberg and Robert D. Webber in their book, *Stretch Out Your Hand,* to the group.

   The practice of healing prayer will always be something experienced before it is understood, known by the heart before it is grasped by the mind. *The concerns of the scientific worldview, legitimate and appropriate in themselves, need not become blocks to ex-*

*ploring healing prayer. What are needed for that jour-
ney are an open mind and heart and a trust in God our
good creator and healer.*[33]

3. Encourage group members to share personal stories that relate how prayer and healing go together.

4. Discuss Matthew H. Gates's hospital story. Someone has said that a coincidence is God's choosing to remain anonymous. Have any group members had significant coincidences that might be related to intentional prayer?

5. Invite group members to have a prayer experience in centering, silence, and listening. Being polite enough to listen to God is a helpful understanding of prayer.

Remove everything from your hands and your lap. Relax as best you can. Breathe slowly and deeply. As you inhale, breathe in the Holy Spirit; as you exhale, let go of tensions, stress, and worry. Do not rush. Relax with God. Encourage each one to say, "I close the door of my spirit to all except the spirit of Christ."

After a few minutes of silence, the leader could gently raise these thoughts to the group:

~ Perhaps you have no agenda other than to be totally in God's presence. If so, simply pray, "Here I am Lord." Then listen.

~ Perhaps you are seeking God's guidance and discernment in a personal matter. Raise the issue to God in prayer and listen.

~ Perhaps you are seeking a healing. Ask God to reveal what exactly needs to be healed and what might be your next step in the healing process. Listen.

Take as much time as seems appropriate. Then invite sharing out of the silence. Do not expect everyone or anyone to speak up.

Close by praying in unison this paraphrase of the prayer of St. Francis of Assisi:

> *Gracious, loving, caring God,*
> *Source of all healing and wholeness,*
> *Make us instruments of Your healing.*
> *When we are weak and in pain, help us to rest;*
> *When we are anxious, help us to wait patiently;*
> *When we are fearful, help us to trust in You;*
> *When we are lonely, help us to love;*
> *When we place You apart from us,*
>   *help us to know that You are still near.*
> *Healing God, grant us not so much to demand everything*
>   *from ourselves, as to allow others to help us;*
> *Grant us not so much to seek escape, as to face ourselves*
>   *and to learn the depths of Your love.*
> *For it is in being uncertain and not in control,*
>   *that we find true faith;*
> *In knowing the limits of mind and body,*
> *that we find wholeness of spirit;*
> *In passing through death that we find life*
>   *that lasts forever.*
> *In the name of Christ Jesus, our Savior,*
>   *our Healer, our Lord, we offer ourselves to You.*
> *Amen.*

Chapter Six

Sacramental Therapy

~~~~~~

WHEN JESUS WANTED TO TELL OTHERS about the reality of God's love, the grace of God's forgiveness and mercy, and the mystery of the eternal covenant between God and God's people, he chose common, familiar, everyday items; such as birds, seeds, weeds, flowers, and bushes. Consider four of the ordinary things Jesus used in extraordinary ways: bread, wine, hands, and oil.

Holy Communion/Eucharist/Lord's Supper

First, let us focus on the sacramental therapy of the bread and wine of Holy Communion. For many Christians, the worship experience that consistently brings them into personal contact with Jesus Christ in the sacrament of Holy Communion. Its other names include the Lord's Supper or the Eucharist (from the Greek word for "thanksgiving"). This sacrament is one of Christ's healing gifts to his church.

When we gather at the Lord's table to participate in the sacrament of Holy Communion, we have a unique opportunity to bring our personal insufficiencies to the all-sufficient Christ, to bring our lack of wholeness to receive his complete wholeness.

Think of Holy Communion as sacramental therapy—as Christ's means of grace, communicating health, wholeness, and salvation. In this context, the word *therapy* means any helpful method or treatment that assists, enhances, or facilitates the healing process. The word *sacrament* means a holy moment, event, sign, or action in which God's spirit is the primary, dynamic factor. The Apostle Paul faithfully passed on this unique spiritual therapy to the New Testament churches:

1 Corinthians 11:23-26

For I received from the Lord what I also handed on to you, that the Lord Jesus on the night when he was betrayed took a loaf of bread, and when he had given thanks, he broke it and said, "This is my body that is for you. Do this in remembrance of me." In the same way he took the cup also, after supper, saying, "This cup is the new covenant in my blood. Do this, as often as you drink it, in remembrance of me." For as often as you eat this bread and drink the cup, you proclaim the Lord's death until he comes.

1 Corinthians 10:16

The cup of blessing that we bless,
is it not a sharing in the blood of Christ?
The bread that we break,
is it not a sharing in the body of Christ?

Even though this participation, this remembrance, this reenactment is beyond satisfactory words of explanation, the faithful Christian does experience direct contact with the source of life, health, salvation, and wholeness in Holy Communion.

Notice how Paul purposely ties together the Lord's Supper with the life, the death, the resurrection, and the coming again of Christ. Worshipful moments of Holy Communion are dramatic reminders of the total gospel message rooted in the atonement made possible by Christ. Is it not ironic that the worst day in his life, the day he was crucified, is known throughout Christendom as Good Friday?

To be "at one" with God in Christ is to be healed at the deepest and most significant levels. In our daily journey toward wholeness in body, in mind, in spirit, and in all of our human relationships, we need the grace of God as experienced in the sacraments again and again.

Sometimes persons ask the question: How frequently should a Christian participate in Holy Communion? Perhaps the answer is another question: How often do we need to experience the love, mercy, forgiveness, and grace of God in our lives?

We cannot overstate the health-enhancing possibilities of the sacrament of Holy Communion. Christian leaders of worship would do well to help sensitize each congregation to a new level of appreciation. Every eucharistic liturgy has many moments that assist and enhance the healing process; such as, adoration and praise, thanksgiving, prayer, confession, forgiveness, assurance of pardon, holy scripture, meditation, reflection, silence, hymns, and the invitation to come in faith to the Lord's table.

Because our receptivity and attitude are so crucial in cooperating with God's yearning for good health, the traditional "Prayer of Humble Access" can be especially therapeutic:

We do not presume to come to this thy table, O merciful Lord, trusting in our own righteousness, but in thy manifold and great mercies. We are not worthy so much as to gather up the crumbs under thy table. But thou art the same Lord, whose property is always to have mercy. Grant us, therefore, gracious Lord, so to partake of this Sacrament of thy Son Jesus Christ, that we may walk in newness of life, may grow into his likeness, and may evermore dwell in him, and he in us. Amen.[34]

However, the most positive single factor is the total focus on Christ, who is the heartbeat and the source of wholistic, abundant life. One of the subtle and not-so-subtle temptations in healing ministry is to place more faith and trust in those who minister to us rather than in the healing Christ. The Holy Communion liturgy provides a necessary balance. This is the table of Christ; therefore, those who have leadership roles are secondary in the sacred drama. We come to be with Christ, consciously remembering his risen presence as we communicate with his Holy Spirit.

Psalm 34:8
O taste and see that the LORD is good;
  happy are those who take refuge in him.

To participate by faith in the breaking of the bread and in the drinking of the cup is to participate in the very life, spirit, and presence of Christ. To become one with Christ always enhances and promotes health and wholeness.

Listen with your heart to these Christian witnesses who testify to the strong relationship between Holy Communion and healing. Martin Luther, the sixteenth century church reformer, called the Eucharist "the medicine of God" because he knew people who received healing at the Lord's table.

A Christian registered nurse
The Eucharist for me is a spiritual booster shot, an immunization against disease and evil.

Morton Kelsey, an Episcopalian priest, calls the Eucharist a healing sacrament because we receive love (the love of Christ) and then we share this love with others, and that is healing.

Charles de Foucauld
Never miss a [holy] communion through your own fault; communion is more than life, more that all the wealth of the world, more than the whole universe; . . . [Communion is] Jesus. How can you prefer something else to [Jesus]?[35]

A Word about Combining Holy Communion and Prayers for Healing and Wholeness in the Same Worship Service

Some pastors and priests prefer to have personal prayers for healing and wholeness before the sacrament of Holy Communion. Then receiving the bread and the cup can be an act of thanksgiving and affirmation of faith in the healing Christ. Other worship leaders prefer to invite the congregation to come forward to receive Holy Communion followed by remaining at the communion table or railing for the anointing with oil and the laying-on-hands with prayers for personal needs. Which method is more correct, liturgically speaking?

Dr. Hoyt Hickman, an acknowledged authority in the history and practice of Christian liturgies, states that the official rituals of most denominations place the prayers for healing before Holy

94

Communion, including the prayers of intercession, confession, and reconciliation. However, he feels reasons exist to support either practice, and he encourages an experimental attitude. One could see Holy Communion either as sealing and celebrating what has been done in the prayers or as bringing the faithful to a point of greater readiness for healing and wholeness prayer ministry.

The International Order of St. Luke the Physician (OSL) uses both methods in worship services, with prayers for healing and wholeness offered in some services before and in other services after Holy Communion.

Because this ministry of combining Holy Communion and healing prayer is new in many congregations, perhaps the more helpful direction would be for the worship leaders to be flexible and experimental, trying various approaches in order to be more sensitive to the Holy Spirit's movement in Christian worship. By taking an experimental attitude, the ministers can engage the participants in dialogue and evaluation, allowing the body of Christ to share in shaping the liturgy.

Personal Reflection

~~~~~~~~~~~

For you, what is the best part, or the spiritual high moment, of Holy Communion? What consistently happens that inspires your soul?

The statement was made that the sacrament of Holy Communion can be sacramental therapy for each Christian. Can you recall a time of participating in Holy Communion when you experienced a personal healing, blessing, benefit, or improvement in your body, your mind, your emotions, your spirit, or in a personal relationship? Be specific.

Try a spiritual experiment. The next time you participate in Holy Communion, look upon this as a precious moment for you and Christ to be together in a healing experience. As you receive the bread and the wine, visualize the healing touch of Christ reaching out to you. To prepare yourself for this special moment, write down the place, date, and hour of your next opportunity for Holy Communion:

List some of your deep personal needs that you plan to bring to the healing Christ at that next Holy Communion time:

Now, offer a prayer of thanksgiving for your anticipated healing and wholeness blessing.

96

Laying On of Hands or Physical Touch

Next we focus on another sacramental therapy called "laying on of hands" with prayer. We communicate powerful messages through physical touch. We have a natural inclination and tendency to reach out and touch those we wish to greet or to comfort. Our hands transmit healing and caring:

~ The restless child becomes quiet.

~ The distraught person realizes that someone cares.

~ The handshake shows acceptance.

~ A gentle hug conveys love and empathy.

According to the Gospel records, Jesus did not hesitate to use physical touch in communicating God's love. His hands were instruments of hope, help, and healing. However, heed this word of caution. Sometimes Jesus used his hands in healing and sometimes he did not. In several instances, Jesus healed people without laying on hands. He only used physical touch when he sensed that would be appropriate or when people came to him requesting that therapy. His contemporary disciples would do well to follow the same model in healing ministry, using physical touch with permission only.

Personal Reflection
~~~~~~~~~~~~~

As you read these examples of laying on of hands from Jesus' healing ministry, put yourself into each scene. Imagine that you are the one that experienced the physical touch of Jesus' hands in each story, and record:

1. Your feelings before, during, and after he touched you.

2. Why you think Jesus chose to lay on hands in each situation.

Read Matthew 8:1-4.

Read Matthew 8:14-15.

Read Mark 8:22-25.

Read Luke 13:10-17.

The early Christians employed laying on of hands in the ordination of ministers, in the commissioning of missionaries, in receiving the baptism of the Holy Spirit, and in healing. Laying on of hands was one of the basic Christian teachings.

98

Hebrews 6:1-2
Therefore let us go on toward perfection, leaving behind
the basic teaching about Christ, and not laying again the
foundation: repentance from dead works and faith toward
God, instruction about baptisms, laying on of hands, resur-
rection of the dead, and eternal judgment.

Because of the obvious biblical precedent, coupled with our natural desire to reach out to people in need, we should not hesitate to touch gently and lovingly those who ask for healing prayer with laying on of hands.

However, always remember that the focal point is not the hands but the healing Christ. Clergy and laity alike have the privilege of offering their hands, their faith, their love, and their compassion for use by Christ to do his saving, healing work among his people.

The answer to statement 8 in the True/False Quiz is *true*. When we engage in laying on of hands with prayer, we are allowing ourselves to be instruments of God's love, flowing in us and through us to others. Laying on of hands is a tangible expression of the sacramental grace operating in the name of Jesus and for his glory.[36]

Anointing with Oil

Another sacramental therapy is anointing with oil in healing minis-try. In biblical times, oil (often common olive oil) was considered an effective, readily available medicine. Two passages indicate some of the ways persons used oil as a medicinal agent.

Isaiah 1:6
From the sole of the foot even to the head, there is no
soundness in [the body], but bruises and sores and bleed-
ing wounds; they have not been drained, or bound up, or
softened with oil.

Luke 10:30, 33-34
A man was going down from Jerusalem to Jericho, and
fell into the hands of robbers, who stripped him, beat

him, and went away, leaving him half dead. . . . But a
Samaritan while traveling came near him; . . . and
bandaged his wounds, having poured oil and wine on
them.

Jesus, who told this story of the "good Samaritan," also instructed his apostles to use oil in their ministry with others.

Mark 6:7, 13
He called the twelve and began to send them out two by
two, and gave them authority over the unclean spirits. . . .
They cast out many demons, and anointed with oil many
who were sick and cured them.

A generation of Christians later, anointing people with oil when praying for healing continued in the life of the New Testament churches.

James 5:14, 16
Are any among you sick? They should call for the elders of
the church and have them pray over them, anointing them
with oil in the name of the Lord. . . . pray for one another,
so that you may be healed. The prayer of the righteous is
powerful and effective.

This counsel of James strongly implies that medicine and prayer go together and that God uses both kinds of therapies in the healing process, the medical and the spiritual. The answer to statement 7 in the True/False Quiz is *true.*

Scripture clearly teaches that oil is an authentic biblical symbol for healing. The small amount of oil used in a public healing service or in a prayer group has no healing effectiveness of its own. The oil does not heal. Rather, anointing the forehead, while making the sign of the cross with the thumb or forefinger, is a sacramental symbol pointing beyond itself to the presence of the healing Christ. Some Christians, when engaged in this ministry, relate the oil to the anointing presence of the Holy Spirit or to Christ who is God's anointed Messiah.

Actually the sacramental therapy of anointing with oil combines four powerful symbols:

1. The oil is a biblical symbol for healing.
2. Making the sign of the cross is a reminder of the centrality of Christ in healing.
3. Naming the holy Trinity or the name of Jesus in the act of anointing invokes the Holy Spirit.
4. The gentle touch in the act of anointing is a form of laying on of hands.

Yes, the sacramental therapy of anointing with oil, based on New Testament teaching and practice, continues to be valid and appropriate in today's churches.

Personal Reflection

~~~~~~~~~~~~~

Reflect on this chapter's reading, which highlights several forms of sacramental therapy. Then answer the following questions.

1. What was new and thought-provoking?

2. What questions did it raise in your mind that need further research?

3. What personal action goals did it prompt you to name?

Group Reflection/Discussion Guide

Chapter Six: Sacramental Therapy

~~~~~~~~~~~~~~~~~~~~~~~~~

1. Consider Holy Communion as sacramental therapy. Invite the group members to share personal experiences in response to these two questions:

    ~ For you, what is the best part or the spiritual high moment in Holy Communion?

    ~ Can you recall a time of participating in Holy Communion when you experienced a personal healing in your body, your mind/emotions, your spirit, or a personal relationship?

2. Has anyone in the group had the experience of laying on of hands with prayer? If so, describe the setting. Share feelings and thoughts.

3. Relax while experiencing another form of laying on of hands. Invite the group to stand in a circle, facing the center. Then ask everyone to turn 90 degrees to the right and place his or her hands on the shoulders of the person in front. Proceed to take a few moments to massage gently the neck, shoulders, and back area. Then turn 180 degrees and repeat the process for a few moments. Now exchange handshakes and hugs and talk about those laying on of hands experiences. NOTE: Be sure to explain this exercise in advance, giving group members the choice of participating.

4. Demonstrate anointing with oil. You will need a volunteer from the group and a small amount of oil (use olive oil or sweet oil). Invite the volunteer to sit in a chair facing the group. The leader

will then anoint the person's forehead with oil using the thumb or forefinger, while making the sign of the cross.

Use the person's first name and say the following words: "___(name)___, I anoint you in the name of the Father, the Son, and the Holy Spirit. Receive God's healing grace. Amen."

Or you could say, "___(name)___, I anoint you in the name of Jesus Christ. Receive his healing and be whole. Amen."

Have the volunteer return to his or her seat with your appreciation. Give others in the group the opportunity to anoint and to be anointed.

You may want to discuss the four symbols of anointing (page 101), as well as questions from the group about the use of oil in healing ministry.

5. To fully appreciate sacramental therapy, you need to experience it. Here is a way to begin this particular prayer practice. (NOTE: If any in the group do not feel comfortable participating in the following, they may observe.)

~ Inquire if anyone has a personal need for healing of body, mind, spirit, or relationships for which he or she would like prayer.

~ Invite that person to sit on a chair placed in the middle of the group and to share with the group the specific prayer concern or focus, or give permission to ask for prayer without stating a personal, specific need.

~ All who wish to participate gather around and gently touch the person with loving compassion on the shoulder, back, head, or hands.

~ One of the group members will then anoint the forehead with oil using the procedure outlined in number 4 above.

~ Then have another group member pray, "___(name)___, may the power of Christ's indwelling presence heal you of all infirmities and illnesses of body, mind, spirit, and relationships, so that you may serve him with a loving heart. Amen."

Others in the circle of compassion may desire to offer brief, spontaneous prayers as prompted by the Holy Spirit.

~ If other group members request this prayer ministry, repeat the entire procedure.

~ If it is appropriate, invite the group to discuss this special time of prayer where you combined anointing with oil and laying on of hands.[37]

6. Conclude this session by standing in a circle, holding hands, and praying the Lord's Prayer together.

Chapter Seven

Questions Most Frequently Asked

~~~~~~

WHEN CHRISTIANS GATHER TO STUDY AND DISCUSS healing ministry, many questions inevitably surface. Keep in mind that this list of
seventeen questions and answers is not exhaustive nor complete. It is
intended to encourage ongoing inquiry and research. Although the
heart often knows what the mind cannot express, we are to use our
God-given mental capacities for ongoing investigation and education.

1. Must you have faith to be healed?

> Medical science now is demonstrating that faith is a significant
> factor in the healing process. When we consciously call on God
> who cares, placing our lives and situations within God's com-
> passion, trusting unconditionally in God's love, we send mes-
> sages to our body, mind, and spirit to relax, to let go of worry
> and anxiety. This relaxing releases certain chemicals into the
> body's bloodstream, thereby cooperating with the healing
> process. The role of faith is crucial, and the more we exercise a
> personal faith in God who cares and heals the better the results.
>   However, God is God. God can heal persons who do not
> pray, who do not believe God cares about them, and who would
> not consider themselves to have any kind of faith. God's mercy
> is boundless.

Matthew 5:45
For [God] makes his sun rise on the evil and on the good, and sends rain on the righteous and on the unrighteous.

Some Christians put their trust in having faith in faith rather than in having faith in God. It is most unkind, unfair, and un-Christian to say to another person: "Well, if you just had more faith God would heal you." Or, "The reason you were not healed is because you lacked faith." Human beings are in no position to judge if another person does or does not have faith. Only God knows that. It is an act of faith for a person to request prayer or to dial a phone number seeking help. Let us not put the full responsibility for faith on the sick person, but let us be sure that persons of faith surround the sick person.

Jesus, without question, had faith in God to heal. It could have been his faith that activated the healing process when persons of little or no faith came to him for ministry. This is also true of Christians who serve on prayer teams today. Their faith in the healing God is critical. Christians who sit in the pews—uncomfortable with up-front leadership roles—who are faithful intercessors, believing that prayer makes a difference, are also key participants in effective healing ministries.

We can enlist the homebound church members who are persons of prayer and faith. Ask them to pray for the ministry teams and for those who seek healing and wholeness. When you analyze the healing events in the life of Jesus and in the life of the church today, faith is always present in someone but not necessarily in the one seeking help.

Mark 2:5
When Jesus saw their faith, he said to the paralytic, "Son, your sins are forgiven."

2. Why are all people not healed?

Persons who raise this frequently asked question usually mean physical healing. Popular thinking either sees physical health as the essence of life or ignores wholistic human nature, disregarding spiritual health, mental/emotional health, and healthy relationships.

God desires good physical health for us. However, under the best of circumstances good physical health is temporary. When we have employed all available help, including spiritual therapy; and the body's health continues to degenerate, we are faced with a mystery. We simply do not know why some are healed and some are not healed physically. Nevertheless, God is faithful and brings blessings, benefits, and improvements in other areas of our being when the physical self weakens.

Do we not tend to recite the worst case scenario when discussing healing ministry? If we can name one person whose health situation definitely improved when the best spiritual therapy was combined with the best medical therapy, that should be motivation enough to keep on keeping on as faithful, compassionate disciples of the healing Christ.

Ponder these conclusions by Dr. Albert E. Day after a long life of Christian ministry:

> *I must confess that the times when God has seemed most near and God's grace most blessed have not always been when someone has been healed of sickness, but in the hours when there was no [physical] healing but that [healing] of the spirit. Then came a glory that transcended all our hopes, and an assurance that death itself could not dilute or destroy. . . .*
>
> *Of this much we are certain: some for whom we pray will experience a physical healing which could not otherwise have been their happy lot; others will enter into a blessed, conscious comradeship with God; . . . [but] all will know that the church and its ministers deeply care for them, feel their pains, share their griefs. The church will become "a fellowship of those who bear the mark of pain," which is, strangely enough, a fellowship of unique joy.*[38]

3. Is God's intentional will for all human beings to have good health in body, mind, spirit, and relationships?

Yes! Here are four kinds of evidence that support an affirmative answer:

~ God's good creation as described in Genesis 1 and 2.

~ The natural ability of the body to heal itself twenty-four hours every day.

~ The intentional healing ministry of Jesus, which dealt with the whole person.

~ The discoveries and resources of the health care professions.

Statement 3 of the True/False Quiz is *true*. We can translate the Hebrew word for *will* as "yearn." Even though God yearns for the best possible life for all people, God does not make it happen mechanically. Human freedom and human yearnings are too often contrary to God's highest desires.

When we pray for recovery from disease, sickness, and brokenness in body, mind, spirit, and relationships, we are affirming that God is on the side of health and is waiting patiently for human receptivity to spiritual assistance. This means that prayer for healing is human effort—prompted by the Holy Spirit—to cooperate with God's trustworthy will.

Consequently, one does not need to add the "if" clause to prayers for healing and wholeness as in the prayer: "O God, help and heal our loved one, if it be thy will."

When we offer prayers for thanksgiving, forgiveness, peace, and salvation, we do not add the "if" clause. We believe God is one hundred percent in favor of these requests, as well as prayers for healing of body, mind, spirit, and relationships. Perhaps the better way to pray would be like this: "O God, help and heal our loved one, according to your will, your yearning, and your loving desire."

4. Before beginning public healing services in the church, do we need to be certain that someone in the church has the gift of healing?

No! The Holy Spirit's gifts of healing (1 Corinthians 12:9) are not a requirement for effective healing ministry. Healing gifts are a plus but not a prerequisite. Gifts of healing are like icing on the cake. Icing is nice but not necessary. We already have the cake, the body of Christ, the church. Statement 6 of the True/False Quiz is *false*.

The healing ministry of the church is primarily a ministry of obedience to Jesus Christ and of compassion for people. The head of the church, Jesus Christ, will use our faith, our love, our compassion to help and to heal people whether or not we have certain gifts of healing.

Consider this positive statement by Reverend Donald Bartow, a Presbyterian minister who conducts healing services in local churches:

> *The charismatic gift of healing is not a requirement for the Ministry of Healing, but faithfulness on the part of each Christian is the indispensable factor. No special gift of healing is needed for one to begin the Spiritual Healing Ministry because our aim is to lead all to the Great Physician, Jesus Christ. It is not our ability but our availability that is desired. Jesus Christ will do the work and supply the power.*[39]

On the other hand, the Holy Spirit endows all Christians with gifts for ministry and for building up the body of Christ. The New Testament names at least twenty different spiritual gifts. All Christians are encouraged to discover and to use their spiritual gifts.

(See Appendix C for recommended resources on spiritual gifts.)

5. What are the basic qualifications for Christians to engage in healing ministries?

> *Francis MacNutt,*
> *You don't have to have any special gift. Just love Jesus and pray for persons—and healing happens. . . . That way seems to work as well as the fantastic gifts of famous faith healers.*[40]

Referring to Number 4 above, the basic qualifications are these:

~ Obedience to Jesus Christ, who instructed his followers to continue all of his ministries. (See Matthew 28:18-20 and John 14:12-15.)

~ Compassion and love for other people. (See Matthew 22:39 and John 15:12.)

6. Is healing ministry in competition with medical science?

Medicine and psychology alone cannot meet our total health needs. We must address the spiritual dimension in the healing process also. Therefore, competition is inappropriate and cooperation is the goal between medical science and the church community. An active healing ministry does not eliminate the need for the medical insights and practices of our day. God uses these therapies to alleviate human pain and illnesses. Healing ministry is not a substitute for medicine but adds a necessary factor in our pilgrimage toward health and wholeness. Church-based ministries work with and not against the resources of medical science, welcoming close relationships with all in the healing professions.

Many persons in the health professions realize and acknowledge the great value of faith and religious beliefs in recovering from illnesses and in maintaining the good health of themselves and others.

Arthur Walker, M.D., Waverly, Tennessee
I believe all healing is of God, whether it comes via a physician or surgeon, a member of the clergy, the fervent prayer of a layperson, or when elders of the church anoint with oil and pray for recovery. In my daily practice, I see many examples of how God has provided means of recovery when we have damaged our bodies. God not only created us but built within us a fantastic repair system. Truly we are wonderfully made.[41]

John H. Genrich, M.D., Colorado Springs, Colorado
I think you should [pray]. I'm only the helper.[42]
[In response to the request of a young couple to have prayer with their newborn baby who had a serious heart problem]

Bernie S. Siegel, M.D., New Haven, Connecticut
I believe there is no disease whose treatment cannot be enhanced by a doctor who knows how to inspire and guide patients and so to bring into play the body's internal healers. It is when I can help my patients find what Schweitzer called "the doctor within"—when I play coach, as one of my patients put it—that I am most fulfilled in my role as doctor and I serve my patients best. We become a team with joint participation and responsibility.[43]

Doctors do not heal us; rather they work with and facilitate the healing process that God places within each human being. Likewise, the compassionate, praying Christian is a spiritual health care provider, not a spiritual health cure giver. Only God can cure and heal the body, the mind, the spirit, and relationships.

7. How do we get the medical community, especially doctors, active in healing ministry?

Begin in your own congregation and surrounding community by identifying those church members who are health care providers (doctors, nurses, therapists, counselors, administrators, pharmacists, and so forth). Meet with them individually to learn how they integrate their personal faith and their professional life. Share your concern for a wholistic Christian healing ministry. Discuss possibilities for churchwide or small-group programs. One helpful format is to have a panel of presenters (health care professionals), who share their Christian witness, followed by open forum discussion.

An increasing number of health care professional persons are looking for ways to combine their unique medical experiences and Christian commitment in the ongoing ministries of their churches. To learn of other models that bring together the medical community and the church contact:

Health Ministries Association
2427 Country Lane
Poland, Ohio 44514
Phone: 1-800-852-5613

8. What is the purpose of fasting in relationship to healing?

Fasting is a spiritual discipline recommended by Jesus and encouraged in both the Old Testament and the New Testament. The Bible has nearly one hundred references to fasting, for a variety of reasons. Jesus directly links fasting to healing when he speaks to his disciples after healing an epileptic boy.

Mark 9:29, KJV
This kind can come forth by nothing, but by prayer and fasting.

112

Benefits from fasting include these:

~ Directing our attention away from our personal needs to God's meaning and purpose in life, thus clarifying our priorities and ambitions.

~ Sensitizing us to the needs of others and to getting in touch with the motivation to serve.

~ Putting our life and outlook in a healthier, less hectic, Christlike perspective.

Why can voluntary abstinence from food and/or drink—either partially or totally—for a temporary period have a profound spiritual impact? One must experience fasting before one can begin to realize and explain the benefits. Contact your local Christian bookstore for resources on fasting.

9. Are we approaching a time when all churches will offer active, effective, wholistic healing ministries?

Yes! Some religious observers say that a majority of churches will be offering intentional healing ministries by the year 2000. They base this prediction on the dramatic increase of healing ministries in so-called mainstream or traditional churches. Actually in certain parts of the world and in certain denominations, that reality is already present. Statement 5 in the True/False Quiz can be either *true* or *false*, depending on where you live and which church you attend.

10. What about exorcism and deliverance in healing ministry?

When it comes to dealing with the reality of evil, many churches go to one of two extremes:

~ Some tend to ignore evil, making it an unmentionable subject from the pulpit and in the classrooms.

~ Some overreact and blame evil spirits for every problem imaginable.

Taking our cue from Jesus, we can believe that the spirit world is real. The kingdom of God is a spiritual realm where God is in complete charge of everyone and everything. However, God's kingdom has not come fully on earth as it is in heaven. For this reason, Jesus cautioned all who claim him as Lord and Savior that Satan (the devil or the evil one) will do whatever is required to oppose God's plans. Notice that the word *evil* is *live* spelled backwards. The opposite of life, goodness, and eternal values is evil. This is why Jesus taught us to pray the petition in his model prayer often.

> ### Matthew 6:13, RSV
> *Deliver us from evil.*

Because Christ is risen and is present throughout the universe; here on planet earth, through the Holy Spirit, we can call on Christ to help us when we encounter evil. Simply breathing and saying the name of Jesus is one powerful spiritual therapy. The New Testament wisely cautions us.

> ### 1 Peter 5:8
> *Discipline yourselves, keep alert. Like a roaring lion your adversary the devil prowls around, looking for someone to devour.*

> ### Ephesians 6:10-12
> *Be strong in the Lord and in the strength of his power. Put on the whole armor of God, so that you may be able to stand against the wiles of the devil. For our struggle is not against enemies of blood and flesh, but against the rulers, against the authorities, against the cosmic powers of this present darkness, against the spiritual forces of evil.*

In healing ministry we need to make a distinction between exorcism and deliverance. Exorcism is a form, an ecclesiastical ritual intended to release someone who is totally possessed by an evil entity. Total possession by evil is rare, and exorcisms are uncommon. Before proceeding with an exorcism to expel possible evil spirits, common sense strongly recommends investigation of other possible problematic causes. Is there

~ a medical problem?

~ a genetic disorder?

~ a multiple personality?

~ a chemical imbalance?

~ an abused and wounded past?

~ another treatable situation?

Use exorcism only after eliminating all other possible causes and employing other kinds of therapies.

Deliverance ministry, on the other hand, frees a person who is not *possessed* but is *oppressed* by an evil spirit. When prayers for inner healing of a wounded, painful past are ineffective, deliverance ministry may be the needed therapy. Evil spirits have a subtle (and at times, not so subtle) way of trying to control certain areas of weakness within some human beings, causing them to feel or to be oppressed.

The Holy Spirit's gift of discernment is crucial for those Christians engaged in the ministries of exorcism and deliverance. Being able to discern the spirits and to know how to proceed are critical. (Consult Appendix C for recommended resources.)

For the Christian, the best protection from evil influences is to saturate oneself frequently with God's means of grace (Holy Communion; prayer; Bible reading and study; Christian worship; and active participation in the body of Christ, the church).

11. How significant is forgiveness in healing ministry?

Very significant! Consider these points. Forgiveness is

~ a key to good health

~ one of Jesus' most mentioned topics

~ expressed in many ways, as taught by Jesus

~ learned behavior contrary to basic human nature

~ a strength, not a weakness

~ the means to forgive the person and to let go of and to forget the pain

~ a decision of the mind, not an emotion of the heart

~ a process not an event, taking time not to be rushed

~ a benefit to the forgiver as much and sometimes more than to the one being forgiven

~ expected to be a lifestyle of Jesus' followers

Colossians 3:13
Bear with one another and, if anyone has a complaint against another, forgive each other; just as the Lord has forgiven you, so you also must forgive.

Forgiveness is one of the unique and powerfully effective spiritual therapies given to the church and offered regularly by all churches. As we say, hear, and receive through the Holy Communion liturgy, "In the name of Jesus Christ, you are forgiven! Glory to God." (For recommended resources on forgiveness and inner healing consult Appendix C, especially by Flora Wuellner; Doris Donnelly; and Dennis Linn, et al.)

116

12. What is meant by being slain in the spirit?

Sometimes when persons come forward for healing prayer, the presence and the power of the Holy Spirit so fills them with a heightened awareness that their physical energy fades, their legs cannot support their weight, and they appear to fall to the floor—thus the term *being slain in the spirit*.

Francis MacNutt recommends getting rid of the word *slain*, which connotes violence. He prefers to call this phenomenon "being overcome by the spirit" in order "to rest in the Spirit." These terms more adequately describe what actually happens. Resting in the spirit can last from a few seconds to several hours. Furthermore, it is not a sign that a person is necessarily healed, although many are.

We can observe some positive results when persons "rest in the Spirit." Resting in the Spirit

~ demonstrates God's power and peace.

~ is an intimate experience of God's presence.

~ can facilitate conversion or repentance.

~ creates an environment for healing of all kinds.

13. What is the role of the laity in healing ministry?

Laypersons in our churches often are motivated to do more than sit passively in the pews, especially when Christ touches, blesses, saves, and heals. "Pastor, what can I do to serve and to help?" is a natural response.

When laypersons come forward with offers to assist in healing ministry, they feel a leading of the Holy Spirit but sometimes express a lack of training and experience. One pastor, when approached by motivated but hesitant laity asks,

"Have you been baptized?"

"Yes."

"Well, claim your baptism. You belong to Christ. You are Christ's representative. Simply offer yourself in his

117

obedient service. Out of compassion for others, help people get in touch and stay in touch with Christ. That's the heart of it all."

The wise pastor will insist that laypersons who are growing spiritually and who are respected in the community be visible in up-front leadership. Team ministry is preferred to solo ministry. Team ministry communicates the message that laity and clergy together make up the body of Christ, and it also provides opportunities for laity to use their spiritual gifts and talents in serving Christ.

Some Christian denominations consider the act of anointing with oil for healing a sacrament—only to be administered by the ordained elders and deacons. However, other faith traditions consider elders and deacons to be specifically appointed lay leaders in the local church. Consequently, when interpreting James 5:14, persons often raise the question: Who were the elders then and who are the elders now?

James 5:14
Are any among you sick? . . . Call for the elders of the church and have them pray over them, anointing them with oil in the name of the Lord.

When the Epistle of James was written, the development of various functions of ministry had not reached a uniform standard throughout Christianity but was in process.

> *The evidence of the first five Christian centuries gives the impression that anointing the sick . . . was practiced by the laity, and that the clergy at least did not discourage this practice. . . . [John] Chrysostom [345–407 A.D.] tells how in his day men and women would take oil out of the lamps in the churches, carry it home and apply it to sick persons.*[44]

Perhaps an acceptable substitute for the word *elders* in James 5:14 could be "spiritual leaders." This term is more inclusive, meaning the clergy and the lay leadership of the churches. Healing ministry is not the private domain of the clergy.

118

14. What about the New Age movement and Christian healing ministries?

The New Age movement is perhaps more a product of the media than of its own roots. The spectacular elements have caught attention and become identified as the movement itself. Some critics say it all began in the garden of Eden (Book of Genesis) when Adam and Eve rebelled against God and tried to achieve independence from God. In recent time the New Age movement became more visible in the 1960s, 1970s, and 1980s. Actually this movement is a collection of several philosophies and spiritualities under one banner—something of a spiritual smorgasbord. Some new agers believe in reincarnation, and some do not. Others lean heavily on astrology, and some do not.

Diverse teachings of this movement include the following:

~ The powers of the mind can create reality and the kind of world we want to live in.

~ Salvation comes by special or secret knowledge, very similar to the "gnosticism heresy" in the New Testament era and beyond.

~ Channeling is the communication of information to or through a physically embodied human being from a source that is said to exist on some level or dimension other than the physical.

~ Evil is not real.

~ Humanity-as-savior replaces Christ-as-Savior.[45]

Spirituality without Christ is one way to describe the New Age movement that seems to attract people who are seeking spiritual experiences beyond the norms of traditional Christianity. In a world grown increasingly impersonal, computerized, and highly technological, the New Age movement has served to awaken many persons to their spiritual quest for something beyond consumer goods.

Here is an opportunity for the churches to offer the living, risen Christ as the name and power above all others and who is able to meet all human needs. Here is an unprecedented moment in human history to present all of the ministries of the gospel: teaching, preaching, and healing.

Those who have the potential and inclination to be attracted to the New Age movement need to meet Jesus Christ, who is the same yesterday, today, and forever (Hebrews 13:8).

> *Mark 12:24*
> *Is not this the reason you are wrong, that you know neither the scriptures nor the power of God?*

> *John 8:31-32*
> *If you continue in my word, you are truly my disciples; and you will know the truth, and the truth will make you free.*

15. Are some ways of praying more effective in healing ministry?

Granted, healing frequently accompanies prayer, and healing is often the result of prayer. However, one cannot conclude that the prayer or the praying are the healing factors. Prayer is a vehicle that carries human communication and desire to God. Prayer is also the vehicle by which God communicates with human beings.

Because we are sometimes perplexed, confused, and do not know how to proceed in prayer, Paul wrote these words to guide us:

> *Romans 8:26-27*
> *The Spirit helps us in our weakness; for we do not know how to pray as we ought, but that very Spirit intercedes with sighs too deep for words. And God, who searches the heart, knows what is the mind of the*

120

Spirit, because the Spirit intercedes for the saints according to the will of God.

This scriptural teaching removes prayer for healing from the need to be liturgically correct. The mechanics and methods of praying are secondary issues in healing ministry (silent or spoken, time, length, body posture, location, praying in tongues or not praying in tongues, solo or group prayer, written or extemporaneous prayers, and so forth).

The Orthodox Christians teach three ways of praying:

~ Prayer of the lips—forming words and speaking aloud.

~ Prayer of the mind—thinking prayer thoughts or meditation.

~ Prayer of the heart—no agenda other than to be with God in silent contemplation.

Each of these forms is valid and appropriate. Keep in mind that our total reliance is on God who has revealed through the life and ministry of Jesus a personal concern for the whole person.

When it comes to effective prayer in healing ministry, begin by reminding yourself that you are a child of God who loves you and who loves the ones for whom you are praying. Then claim the promise of Christ.

Matthew 28:20
Remember, I am with you always.

Then proceed to pray as the Holy Spirit leads you. When we pray, we are demonstrating our inner motivation to cooperate with God's good will and to give God permission to move in loving, healing, saving ways. Therefore, statement 4 in the True/False Quiz is *true.*

Every prayer you and I pray is an act of healing and wholeness.

When we pray, we are saying "yes" to God and are more receptive to experiencing God's desires for each of us.

16. Is there a direct relationship between sin and sickness?

A relationship can exist but not in every situation. Obviously human beings bring on much of their own illness by making poor choices. Some medical research reports that seventy-five percent of all deaths in the US before age sixty-five are premature and caused by personal, unhealthy lifestyle habits.

Others often experience sickness and suffering as a consequence of someone else's sins. This fallen, broken, imperfect world is a respecter of no one. Healing services offered in churches need to give the worshipers regular opportunities to examine personal lives, to confess sin, to receive forgiveness, and to experience the assurance of pardon in the name of Jesus Christ.

Some persons come to healing services, primarily praying for release from pain and suffering of physical illnesses. They may be overlooking the need for healing of their relationships with God and other people. Some people are not healed physically, mentally/emotionally, spiritually, or in human relationships because they refuse to acknowledge sin or to let go of sin and guilt with God's help. In Christian counseling, wholistic therapy always explores the possibility of our personal sin being a barrier in the healing process.

In some of Jesus' healings, he did not mention the need of forgiveness, sensing that the person's illness was not sin-related. (For examples see Mark 1:29-31; Matthew 9:20-22; Matthew 9:27-31.) However, in other Gospel records, Jesus apparently sensed a direct cause-and-effect relationship between sin and illness. In these cases, he assisted the person in being forgiven of sin, as well as in being healed in other ways. (For examples see Mark 2:1-12; John 5:1-15; John 8:1-11.)

All illness is not due to sin, but experience dictates the necessity of frequent personal examination of conscience and confession of sins. To be insensitive to this critical area of our lives is to overlook a crucial factor in our total well-being and good health.

17. What is unique about Christian healing ministry?

In the midst of a seminar on the topic "Healing and Prayer," a man raised his hand, identified himself as a Jewish physician and declared, "Christians do not have a monopoly on healing!" The medical doctor spoke the truth. Our Creator God has provided numerous ways and delivery systems to say to the created ones: "I love you. I care about your life and health. I have many kinds of therapy (help) and untold numbers of therapists (helpers) all over the world, in every culture, race, and religion."

The only unique and unparalleled resource for healing in Christianity is Christ himself. The question is not, Are there resources for healing in non-Christian religions? Obviously the answer is, "Yes, there are many."

The Christian makes this statement: Because I am committed to Jesus Christ as Lord and Savior, I know that he is risen and that his Holy Spirit is actively working in today's world, continuing all of his ministries (teaching, preaching, and healing). For the Christian who affirms the previous statement, the question then is this: When I become sick or unhealthy, when my body/mind/spirit/relationships get out of balance, when I experience disharmony and lack of wholeness; do I intentionally, with faith, trust, and thanksgiving, turn to Jesus Christ for the wholistic healing that he desires for me and for all of his followers? Do I call on and use all of the spiritual therapies Christ has placed within the life of every church? Jesus sums up the uniqueness about Christian healing ministry when he addresses all God's people.

John 10:10
I came that they may have life, and have it abundantly.

Personal Reflection

~~~~~~~~~~~~~

1. Having read this chapter on Questions Most Frequently Asked, list those questions about healing ministry that you still are asking and for which you are seeking further light and clarification. Beside each question, list some possible resources that could help you (persons, books, continuing education opportunities, churches).

My Personal Questions   *Possible Answer Resources*

2. Reflect on your entire study of *An Adventure in Healing and Wholeness*, and list your most significant insights and learnings.

3. Conclude with an unhurried time of prayer. Begin by thanking God that all of the ministries of Jesus Christ are available today (teaching, preaching, and healing).

Then open your total being to the Holy Spirit's direction, asking what might be your next step in becoming more active and intentional in healing ministry. Record your thoughts and feelings.

When you are ready, offer a prayer for obedience and courage in being a faithful disciple of Jesus Christ.

Group Reflection/Discussion Guide

Chapter Seven: Questions Most Frequently Asked

~~~~~~

1. Review the seventeen questions and answers, inviting comments by the group members. Keep in mind that this list of questions is not exhaustive nor are the answers complete. This chapter is intended to stimulate further investigation and inquiry.

2. Look at the "Personal Reflection" (page 124). Invite the group members to share their personal questions and possible answer resources.

3. Look again at the "Group Reflection/Discussion Guide" for Chapter One: An Overview of the Healing Ministry. Refer to your notes for Number 3, where you discussed the ways to "offer a positive understanding of healing ministry" (page 25). Having now completed your personal and group study of *An Adventure in Healing and Wholeness*, in what ways do you need to revise your strategies and action plans? List two or three practical and possible next steps for your congregation.

4. Close with prayer.

Appendices

Some Practical Matters

~~~~~~~~~~~~~~~~~~~~~~~~~~~~

Taking the Next Steps

As you reflect on your spiritual journey, pray for the guidance of the Holy Spirit in selecting your next steps. Carefully look over these possibilities. Be realistic. Be specific. Place check marks by those steps that will challenge you to move ahead in becoming more healthy and whole in body, mind, and in your relationship with others.

Some next steps in my personal life

___ Renew my commitment to Jesus Christ.

___ Commit my life to Jesus Christ for the first time.

___ Take personal time each day for solitude, prayer, Bible reading.

___ Offer grace at mealtimes.

___ Begin family devotions.

___ Develop a physical fitness program.

___ Undertake a nutritious and balanced diet program.

___ Make and keep the doctor's appointment I have been putting off.

___ Forgive someone who hurt me deeply, with God's grace and help.

___ Participate actively in the life and ministry of my church.

___ Name another possible next step in my personal life.

Some next steps in the life of my church

___ Organize a study/discussion group around the topic of healing and wholeness ministries.

___ Form or join an intercessory prayer group.

___ Visit persons in hospitals, homes, and retirement centers.

___ Volunteer to be on a special committee to plan and sponsor an annual emphasis on healing and wholeness in my church with a guest leader.

___ Volunteer to be on a standing committee that would identify, plan, promote, sustain, and encourage health and wholeness ministries year-round in my church.

___ Encourage my pastor and worship planners to offer regular opportunities for the ministry of healing prayer and volunteer to assist in appropriate ways.

___ Name another possible next step in the life of my church.

After naming your next steps, commit them to God in prayer. Share them with another Christian who will be supportive, affirming, and encouraging. Then begin taking your next steps.

Ways to Begin Healing Services

The following suggestions for getting started come from the book *Blessed to Be a Blessing: How to Have an Intentional Healing Ministry in Your Church*.[46] For more details see *Blessed to Be a Blessing*, Chapter Four, "The Public Healing Service."

Getting Started

Prior to announcing the first public healing service, the minister needs to have informed the congregation carefully about his or her interest in the healing ministry. This sharing of interest may come through a series of sermons based on any of the several biblical healing events, pastoral articles in the church newsletter, and/or informal conversations with adult groups in the church.

Crucial in the preparation stage is the discovery of church members who are interested in and receptive to learning more about healing ministry. Pastors can discover these persons by offering short-term study groups on the subject or simply by inviting interested persons to contact the pastor for informal, exploratory conversations. Healing services that are primarily initiated, organized, sustained, and solely led by the pastor will have limited influence on the ongoing life of the congregation. The healing ministry must involve lay leadership in every facet of the healing ministry. The wise pastor will offer training and leadership opportunities for motivated, concerned laypersons.

Consider taking an experimental approach to intentional healing ministry. Set a time limit and establish ways to evaluate the experiment. Congregational governing bodies and official boards are more likely to cooperate on this basis. Set an initial time frame of three to four months assuring that evaluations be made. Toward the end of the experimental period, return to the governing body of the church with reportable data and specific recommendations.

Deciding on Service Format

After deciding to begin, other questions arise for consideration and action:

~ What type of worship service should we have? formal or informal?

~ Should we have Holy Communion, anointing oil, and a printed order of service?

~ How frequently should we hold the services?

~ When should we hold the services?

~ Where shall we hold the services?

~ Who will lead the services?

You can gain a lot of information by visiting, observing, and participating in healing services held in other churches. In addition to the inspiration received, these visits will generate learning and ideas. However, do not copy a congregational worship style that differs radically from your own. Begin with the familiar. Design a basic liturgy that participants can understand and accept.

It is always appropriate, especially in the beginning stages of a public healing ministry, to explain to the gathered body of Christ what you are doing and why you are doing it. This teaching time can be the homily, part of the opening greeting and remarks, or a brief introduction to various components of the liturgy. The goal is to put the worshipers "at ease," not to foster "dis-ease" in the healing environment.

Attending to Ongoing Concerns

Give attention to frequency, location, and time of the services. I strongly advocate weekly healing services for these reasons:

1. Monthly healing services tend to communicate a negative message. "Healing services are not as important as weekly choir practice, Sunday school, and Sunday morning services."
2. It is too difficult for many people to remember meetings that are held only on certain weeks of the month.
3. Personal problems, tragedies, and dilemmas cannot always wait for the next monthly or quarterly healing service. They need to be immersed with spiritual therapy as soon as possible.

Attendance at local church healing services often falls below the expectation level of the persons in charge. You will find yourself quoting Jesus frequently:

Matthew 18:20
Where two or three are gathered in my name, I am there among them.

The number of persons who attend may look like a small-group experience, regardless of the membership size of the host church. Our goal is to be faithful and obedient to Christ in offering a regular, well-publicized time for all interested persons to participate in healing ministry opportunities. Some will be there every time; others only when they are facing a crisis. Remember that the healing Christ can use the faith, love, compassion, and the prayers of a few to feed the multitude. An ounce of obedience is worth a ton of Bible study.

Questionnaire Related to Church Healing Services

1. I have attended regularly ___ occasionally ___ once ___

2. I think the healing services should be continued: Yes ___ No ___

3. I like the present time of the services: Yes ___ No ___

4. I could attend more often if these services were held at another time: Yes ___ No ___

5. Here are my suggestions for different times to offer the healing services:

6. The parts of the service I like the best are

7. The parts of the service I like the least are

8. I personally have been helped by this healing ministry:

    ___ spiritually
    ___ emotionally
    ___ physically
    ___ relationships with others
    ___ other ways (please explain)

9. Suggestions for improving the effectiveness of these services:

10. I am interested in attending a short-term study course or a one-day seminar dealing with an in-depth look at the healing ministry of Christ in the church today.
Yes ___ No ___

11. Personal comments and questions:

Signature _____ (optional)

Please return this questionnaire to the church office by __(date)__.
Thank you for your help.[47]

134

Additional Recommended Resources for Getting Started

Don Bartow (a Presbyterian minister) has written and published a wealth of materials related to healing ministry. For a current catalog of resources, contact:

Rev. Don Bartow
Total Living Center
2221 9th Street SW
Canton, OH 44706
Phone 216-455-3663

Albert E. Day (a United Methodist minister), founder of the Disciplined Order of Christ, wrote an excellent teaching text based on his pastoral experiences in conducting healing services in the 1950s called *Letters on the Healing Ministry.* To order *Letters on the Healing Ministry*, contact:

Disciplined Order of Christ
P.O. Box 23617
Nashville, TN 37202-3617

For guidelines on local church healing services, see *Letters on the Healing Ministry*, Appendix 2, "The Ministry to the Sick."

Morton Kelsey (an Episcopal minister), internationally known author and teacher, updated his classic *Healing and Christianity* with a revised, expanded version entitled: *Psychology, Medicine, and Christian Healing* (Harper & Row, 1988). Especially helpful is Chapter Fourteen, "Implementing the Healing Ministry in the Church Today."

Mark A. Pearson (an Episcopal minister), president of the Institute for Christian Renewal, has an excellent section in his book, *Christian Healing: A Practical, Comprehensive Guide* (Fleming H. Revell, 1990). See Chapter 11, "How to Introduce a Healing Ministry into Your Church."

Models for Healing Services

Here are four methods of offering intentional prayers for healing and wholeness in churches:

In-the-Pews: Everyone stays in the pews. The pastor, priest, or worship leader offers intercessory prayers on behalf of the congregation. This intercession often is incorporated into the regular pastoral prayer. The spoken prayer may or may not name specific persons and needs. Some churches invite the congregation to form small groups in the pews for simultaneous intercessory prayer ministry.

Silent Method: Persons requesting prayer are invited to come forward to the communion railing or altar area. They usually kneel; sometimes stand or sit. Individually they receive the ministry of laying on of hands with silent prayer. The person laying on hands may be a clergyperson or a layperson. Anointing oil is optional. The only word spoken is *Amen* at the conclusion of the silent prayer with each person.

United Method: Persons requesting prayer are invited to come forward to the communion railing, altar, or chancel area. They usually kneel. The minister prays with two persons at a time, placing a hand on each head. The spoken prayer is brief and general, similar to a blessing. Anointing oil is optional.

Team Method: Two or three persons serve on a prayer team. Those requesting prayer are invited to come forward to the communion railing or other designated prayer stations. Each one who comes forward has an opportunity to voice his or her specific concern to the prayer team. All on the team lay on hands and join in silent or spoken prayer. Anointing oil is optional.

The sacramental model for healing services is based on the sacrament of Holy Communion. Leaders may offer prayers for healing and wholeness before or after the distribution of the bread and cup. Each of the four prayer methods described above may be incorporated into a Holy Communion liturgy.

Some models currently practiced in churches today:

~ On Holy Communion Sundays, persons desiring the ministry of prayer with laying on hands and anointing oil are invited to come to the last table group .

~ On Holy Communion Sundays, all table groups are offered the ministry of healing prayer after receiving the bread and the cup. A dismissal prayer is offered for those not desiring personal prayer ministry. Others remain for prayer with laying on of hands and anointing oil.

~ Persons desiring the ministry of healing prayer are requested to come forward after the benediction and during the organ postlude. Others are dismissed and leave the sanctuary. Lay prayer teams are usually assigned in advance to be ready to offer prayer ministry.

~ Incorporated into the regular pastoral prayer is a designated prayer time at the altar for those who wish to come forward. As the organ plays quietly in the background, the pastor and lay leaders may pray individually with each one. Others may come to the altar for silent, personal prayer time. Anointing oil is optional.

Many churches offer an abbreviated Holy Communion service with prayers for healing in connection with another worship service or activity in the church.

~ before Sunday school and worship on Sunday mornings

~ between Sunday morning services

~ around noon on Sundays after the other services end

~ midweek Bible study

~ Sunday night services

~ noontime services during the week

~ early on weekday mornings

Here is liturgy for healing services using the silent method of praying. This offering is to all interested persons every Thursday at 11:00 A.M. in the Mt. Washington United Methodist Church, Baltimore, Maryland, sponsored by "The New Life Clinic." The liturgy is announced as the service progresses, lasting fifty to sixty minutes. Holy Communion is not offered. Anointing oil is optional. This order of service has remained the same since the early 1950s when Dr. Albert E. Day and Ambrose and Olga Worrall designed and started this ministry.

> *Organ Music* (begins at 10:45 A.M. for meditation)
> *Greetings, Welcome, Announcements*
> *Hymn* ("Breathe on Me, Breath of God")
> *Scripture Reading*
> *Message* (brief)
> *Pastoral Prayer* (brief)
> *Intercessory Prayer* (Persons write prayer concerns on small cards, which are brought forward by an usher and placed on the altar. After a time of silent intercession, the minister prays over the cards, thanking God in advance for healing and wholeness.)
> *Invitation to Come to the Chancel Railing for Prayers* (Four robed persons—lay and clergy—pray individually with those who come forward, laying on hands with silent prayer.)
> *Concluding Statement* (Invitation to come to fellowship hall for refreshments and fellowship)
> *Benediction*
> *Organ Postlude*

Consult denominational books of worship for other healing services models.

Suggestions for Prayer Ministry Teams

Our role in praying with people is to be a compassionate Christian friend, an instrument of God's healing love and grace. When praying with others it is not necessary to "work up a sweat." The prayer teams are not responsible for the solutions or the answers. Let God do the work. When praying for healing, wholeness, and salvation, we are not begging God to change God's mind; rather, we are giving God permission to work in our lives and in the lives and situations of the ones with whom and for whom we are praying. Prayer teams are cooperating with God's desire and yearning for wholistic health.

Remember, God is the healer! Our role is to love people. God's role is to change people. Let's try not to confuse the two roles.

We can pray with people

~ with or without the laying on of hands

~ with or without anointing oil

~ with formal or informal prayers

~ with silent or spoken prayers

~ with the posture that is most comfortable

In your prayers, use the name for God that is most natural for you. The traditional prayer liturgy suggests that we pray to God the Father, through the Son, in the Holy Spirit. Many Christians feel more at ease simply addressing Jesus in their prayers.

When serving on a prayer team:
1. Have a time of prayer together with your partners before the healing service begins.
2. Discuss your pattern of praying with your partners. Have a plan before the service begins.
3. Consider using this prayer pattern. Remember L-A-P.
   Listen (L): Ask each one who comes to your prayer station, "What is your prayer concern today?" Then listen closely.
   Anoint (A): Anoint the forehead with oil, using the thumb or forefinger, while making the sign of the cross.

Pray (P): The prayer partner who listened to the prayer concern will offer a brief prayer. Other prayers, silent or spoken, may follow as the Spirit leads.

4. Change the sequence if your team prefers to L-P-A or Listen-Pray-Anoint.

5. Lay on hands gently, not heavily. Involve all team members in this endeavor.

6. Be brief in public prayer ministry. It is not necessary to pray long and loud. Keep your prayers private and personal. Confidentiality is crucial. Keep in mind that the prayer does not do the healing. God is the healer. Praying with others for healing, wholeness, and salvation is a holy, special privilege. In an act of faith and obedience, lift up each one into the healing light and love of Jesus Christ.

7. Whisper to persons who come forward, obviously needing extended, unhurried prayer and counseling: "Let's have a brief prayer now, and after the service is over we will get together for continuing ministry." This is a courtesy to the rest of the congregation.

8. Team members who want personal prayers for healing and wholeness will pray with one another after ministering to the congregation.

Sample Prayer Patterns

~ These hands are laid upon you in the name of the Father, the Son, and the Holy Spirit. May the power of God's indwelling presence heal you of all infirmities of mind, body, spirit, and relationships, that you may serve God with a loving heart. Amen.

~ Lord Jesus Christ, strengthen and heal (name of person). May your healing love and power flow into (his or her) life. Banish all pain, sickness, and sin. Give (him or her) the blessings of health in body, mind, spirit, and relationships. We ask these things in your name and give you the glory. Amen.

140

~ Thank you, Lord Jesus, for this time of Holy Communion with you and with one another. We now lift up into your light and love (name of person). Touch (him or her). Bring (him or her) wholeness in body, mind, spirit, and relationships. For doing all of these things and more, we thank you and give you the glory. Amen.

Continuing Education Opportunities in Healing Ministry

~~~~~~~~~~~~~~~~~~~~~~

Opportunities abound for continuing education in healing and wholeness ministries. The following list, while not comprehensive, represents a wide spectrum of theological positions, teaching methods, and practical applications in ministry. *For more detailed information contact these resources directly.*

Aqueduct Conference Center
P.O. Box 17299, Mount Carmel Church Road
Chapel Hill, NC 27516-7299
Phone 919-933-5557
Director: Rev. Tommy Tyson
Offers a variety of retreat and learning experiences led by nationally known guest faculty.

Total Living Center
2221 9th Street SW
Canton, OH 44706
Phone 216-455-3663
Rev. Don Bartow
In addition to conducting seminars and workshops around the world, Don Bartow has written and published a wealth of materials related to local church healing and wholeness ministries from a pastor's experience.

Health Ministries Association
2427 Country Lane
Poland, OH 44514
Phone 1-800-852-5613

> The mission of Health Ministries Association is to enable understanding, cooperation, and new visions for healing and health ministries for all persons in congregations who desire harmony of body, mind, and spirit. This ecumenical networking association publishes a quarterly newsletter: "Health Ministries Connection."

International Order of St. Luke the Physician (OSL)
P.O. Box 13701
San Antonio, TX 78213
Phone 210-492-5222

> Publishes the monthly magazine *Sharing* and sponsors healing ministry missions, retreats, and conferences in the US and Canada. OSL is thoroughly ecumenical and has many local chapters.

The Journal of Christian Healing
Douglas Schoeninger, editor
103 Dudley Avenue
Narberth, PA 19072
Phone 215-667-0460

> This quarterly journal, founded in 1979 by The Association of Christian Therapists, is published by the Institute for Christian Counseling and Therapy and sponsors annual Christian healing conferences.

International Hospital Christian Fellowship
P.O. Box 4004
San Clemente, CA 92672
Phone 714-496-7655

> The Hospital Christian Fellowhsip (H.C.F.) is a worldwide interdenominational organization founded in 1936. H.C.F. ministries include publication of *A New Heart* (magazine), books and literature, retreats and conferences.

Christian Healing Ministries, Inc.
P.O. Box 9520
438 West 67th Street
Jacksonville, FL 32208
Phone 904-765-3332
Directors: Francis and Judith MacNutt
> Offers healing ministry training conferences at the Jacksonville location and throughout the US, Canada, and Europe. Publishes a newsletter that lists many resources, conference dates and locations, and articles related to healing ministries.

National Parish Nurse Resource Center
1800 Dempster Street
Park Ridge, IL 60068
Phone 708-696-8773
> The Parish Nurse or Church Nurse Program is a growing ecumenical movement that encourages nurses to work and minister within their local church communities. The National Parish Nurse Resource Center has been developed

> ~ as a publisher of materials describing the philosophy and work of parish nurses;

> ~ as a convener of annual educational programs where nurses can meet and learn about current developments;

> ~ to provide consultants to churches, hospitals, and other agencies in organizing parish nurse programs.

Institute for Christian Renewal
233 Poquanticut Avenue
North Easton, MA 02356
Phone 508-238-3372
President: Rev. Mark Pearson
> For those ready to move beyond "the entry level," Mark Pearson and staff offer advanced training in Christian healing ministries at the Massachusetts location and throughout the US. The institute also publishes a newsletter that lists helpful information and articles.

The Upper Room
Director of Healing Ministries
P.O. Box 189
Nashville, TN 37202-0189
Phone 615-340-7228

Offers training courses for *An Adventure in Healing and Wholeness* throughout the US, publishes resource books for prayer and healing ministries, and networks (via computer modem) persons and churches interested in healing ministries.

Vineyard Ministries International
P.O. Box 1359
Placentia, CA 92670
Rev. John Wimber

Has published teaching materials and books. Conducts healing ministry missions in the US and other countries.

Mind Body Therapy Associates
800-C Forest Oaks Lane
Hurst, TX 76053
Phone 817-268-4221
Director: Dr. Steven Vazquez

Dr. Vazquez is the developer of Confluent Somatic Therapy. He combines new research in stress, immunology, pain, and chronic illness with advances in the healing arts to make exceptional physical healing practical. Seminars and workshops are presented throughout the US.

Rev. Tilda Norberg
78 Clinton Avenue
Staten Island, NY 10301
Phone 718-273-4941

In addition to conducting spiritual growth retreats and training workshops, Tilda Norberg has written helpful materials that integrate gestalt psychotherapy, spiritual guidance, and healing prayer.

First United Methodist Church
1115 South Boulder
Tulsa, OK 74119
Phone 918-587-9481

Offers annual teaching seminars in healing ministry for clergy and laity. Courses include ministry of inner healing, Christian counseling, Twelve-Step ministries, and small group-counseling.

Appendix C

Recommended Resources

~~~~~~~~~~~~~~~~~~~~~~~~~~~~~~~~~

THIS BIBLIOGRAPHY IS A SAMPLING OF THE CURRENT EXPLOSION of resources for healing and wholeness ministries. Consult your denominational publishers and local book stores for additional publications and programs.

Introduction and Overview of Healing Ministry

Althouse, Lawrence. *Rediscovering the Gift of Healing.* York Beach: Samuel Weiser, 1977.

Bartow, Donald. *Healing Handbook*, Vol. 1. Canton, OH: Total Living Center, 1992.

Day, Albert E. *Letters on the Healing Ministry.* Nashville: Disciplined Order of Christ, 1990.

Glennon, Jim. *How Can I Find Healing?* London: Hodder and Stoughton, 1984.

——. *Your Healing Is Within You.* London: Hodder and Stoughton, 1978.

MacNutt, Francis. *Healing.* Altamonte Springs, FL: Creation House, 1988.

——. *The Power to Heal.* Notre Dame, IN: Ave Maria Press, 1977.

Neal, Emily Gardner. *Celebration of Healing.* Boston, MA: Cowley Publications, 1992.

Sanford, Agnes. *The Healing Light.* St. Paul, MN: Macalester Park, 1947.

Healing Ministry in Church History

Darling, Frank C. *Biblical Healing.* Boulder, CO: Vista Publications, 1989.

——. *Christian Healing in the Middle Ages and Beyond*. Boulder, CO: Vista Publications, 1990.

——. *The Restoration of Christian Healing*. Boulder, CO: Vista Publications, 1992.

Kelsey, Morton T. *Psychology, Medicine, & Christian Healing* (a revised and expanded edition of *Healing & Christianity*). San Francisco: Harper & Row, 1988.

Fasting and Healing

Foster, Richard J. "Fasting," in *Celebration of Discipline*. San Francisco: Harper & Row, 1988.

Ryan, Thomas. *Fasting Rediscovered*. NY: Paulist Press, 1981.

Wallis, Arthur. *God's Chosen Fast*. Fort Washington, PA: Christian Literature Crusade, 1975.

Gifts of the Holy Spirit

Bryant, Charles V. *Rediscovering Our Spiritual Gifts*. Nashville: Upper Room Books, 1991.

Kinghorn, Kenneth C. *Discovering Your Spiritual Gifts*. Grand Rapids, MI: Zondervan Publishing House, 1984.

Wagner, C. Peter. *The Third Wave of the Holy Spirit*. Ann Arbor, MI: Vine Books, 1988.

Harbaugh, Gary L. *God's Gifted People*. Minneapolis, MN: Augsburg Fortress Publishers, 1988.

Having a Healing Ministry in Your Church

Pearson, Mark A. *Christian Healing*. Grand Rapids, MI: Fleming H. Revell Co., 1990.

Stanger, Frank B. *God's Healing Community*. Wilmore, KY: Francis Asbury Society, 1985.

Wagner, James K. *Blessed to Be a Blessing*. Nashville: Upper Room Books, 1980.

Wagner, C. Peter. *How to Have a Healing Ministry without Making Your Church Sick*. Ventura, CA: Regal Books, 1988.

Inner Healing or Healing of Memories

Hollies, Linda H. *Inner Healing for Broken Vessels.* Nashville, TN: Upper
    Room Books, 1992.
Linn, Dennis, Sheila Fabricant Linn, and Matthew Linn. *Healing the
    Eight Stages of Life.* Mahwah, NJ: Paulist Press, 1988.
Seamands, David A. *Healing for Damaged Emotions.* Wheaton, IL:
    Victor Books, 1981.
Wuellner, Flora S. *Prayer, Stress, and Our Inner Wounds.* Nashville, TN:
    Upper Room Books, 1985.
——. *Heart of Healing, Heart of Light.* Nashville, TN: Upper Room
    Books, 1992.
——. "Depth Healing and Renewal through Christ"(audiocassette tape).
    Nashville, TN: Upper Room Books, 1992.

Prayer and Healing

DelBene, Ron. *Into the Light.* Nashville, TN: Upper Room Books, 1989.
——. *The Breath of Life.* Nashville, TN: Upper Room Books, 1992.
Dunnam, Maxie. *The Workbook of Living Prayer.* Nashville, TN: Upper
    Room Books, 1975.
——. *The Workbook of Intercessory Prayer.* Nashville, TN: Upper Room
    Books, 1979.
Norberg, Tilda & Webber, Robert D. *Stretch Out Your Hand* (comes with
    a leader's guide and videotape). NY: United Church Press, 1990.
Wuellner, Flora S. *Prayer and Our Bodies.* Nashville, TN: Upper Room
    Books, 1987.
——. *Prayer, Fear and Our Powers.* Nashville, TN: Upper Room Books,
1989.

Evil, Deliverance, and Exorcism

Green, Michael. *I Believe in Satan's Downfall.* Grand Rapids, MI:
    William B. Eerdmans Publishing Company, 1981.
Green, Thomas H. *Weeds among the Wheat.* Notre Dame, IN: Ave Maria
    Press, 1984.
Peck, M. Scott. *People of the Lie.* NY: Simon & Schuster, 1985.
Sanford, John A. *Evil.* NY: Crossroad Publishing Company, 1981.
Wink, Walter. *Unmasking the Powers.* Minneapolis, MN: Augsburg
    Fortress Publishers, 1986.

Other Healing Ministry Resources

Bakken, Kenneth L. *The Call to Wholeness*. NY: Crossroad Publishing Company, 1985.

Donnelly, Doris. *Learning to Forgive*. Nashville, TN: Abingdon Press, 1982.

Dossey, Larry. *Recovering the Soul*. NY: Bantam Books, 1989.

Groothuis, Douglas R. *Unmasking the New Age*. Downers Grove, IL: InterVarsity Press, 1986.

MacNutt, Francis. *Overcome by the Spirit*. NY: Fleming H. Revell, 1990.

MacNutt, Francis & Judith. *Praying for Your Unborn Child*. NY: Doubleday, 1989.

May, Gerald G. *Addiction & Grace*. San Francisco: HarperCollins, 1991.

Miller, J. Keith. *A Hunger for Healing*. San Francisco: HarperCollins, 1991.

———. *A Hunger for Healing Workbook*. San Francisco: HarperCollins, 1992.

Morris, Danny E. *Yearning to Know God's Will*. Grand Rapids, MI: Zondervan, 1992.

Nouwen, Henri J. M. *The Wounded Healer*. NY: Image Books, 1979.

Pherigo, Lindsey P. *Great Physician, Luke*. Nashville, TN: Abingdon Press, 1991.

Siegel, Bernie S. *Love, Medicine and Miracles*. San Francisco: HarperCollins, 1990.

———. *Peace, Love and Healing*. San Francisco: HarperCollins, 1990.

Weatherhead, Leslie D. *The Will of God*. Nashville, TN: Abingdon Press, 1976.

Periodicals Related to Healing and Wholeness

A New Heart. International Hospital Christian Fellowship, P.O. Box 4004, San Clemente, CA 92672.

Sharing. The International Order of St. Luke the Physician, P.O. Box 13701, San Antonio, TX 78213.

Journal of Christian Healing. Institute for Christian Counseling and Therapy, 103 Dudley Avenue, Narberth, PA 19072.

Weavings. The Upper Room, P.O. Box 189, Nashville, TN 37202.

More Resources

To learn more about a new series of books related to health and medicine in various religious traditions and Christian denominations (Catholic, Reformed, Jewish, Methodist, Anglican, Islamic, Lutheran, Hindu, Christian Science), contact:

> The Park Ridge Center
> 676 North St. Clair, Suite 450
> Chicago, IL 60611

"Is Any Among You Suffering?" (videotape on anointing with oil, 16 minutes), contact:

> Brethren Press
> 1451 Dundee Avenue
> Elgin, IL 60120

Designed for children (elementary age) by John I. Penn
About Caring and Healing (A coloring and activities book about a loving and healing God)
About the Gifts of the Holy Spirit (A coloring and activities book about God, who gives gifts to help us serve others)

Discussion starter booklets for youth & adults by John I. Penn
What Everyone Should Know about Healing
Understanding the Gifts of the Holy Spirit
Order these items directly from
> John I. Penn
> 112 Country Club Drive
> Newark, DE 19711

"A Health Risk Appraisal." (For personal evaluation and education)
> A cooperative project of The Carter Center HRA Program in Atlanta, GA and SEJ Wellth Ministries, Lake Junaluska, NC.
> For information contact:
> > SEJ Wellth Ministries
> > P.O. Box 237
> > Lake Junaluska, NC 28745

"Healing Ministry Network." (Uses computer-based electronic conferencing to give you access to ECUNET, a network of 18 denominations. For sign-up information contact:

> Susan Peek, UMCOM
> P.O. Box 320
> Nashville, TN 37202-0320
> Phone 615-742-5444
> FAX 615-742-5469

For a free catalog that lists all UPPER ROOM books and resources on healing, wholeness, and prayer ministries, contact:

> The Upper Room
> P.O. Box 189
> Nashville, TN 37202-0189

Endnotes

~~~~~~~~~

1. David Hilton, M.D., "Ethics, World View, and Health," an address to the American Public Health Association, 117th Annual Meeting, October 24, 1989.

2. Albert E. Day, *Letters on the Healing Ministry* (Nashville, TN: Disciplined Order of Christ, 1990), 130.

3. James K. Wagner, "Introduction," *Letters on the Healing Ministry*, 9–10.

4. For those who want to research the history of the healing ministry, see Appendix C, "Recommended Resources."

5. Day, *Letters on the Healing Ministry*, 92.

6. Ebb Munden, in his report to the "Consultation on Healing Ministry," Nashville, TN, October 28-30, 1986.

7. Day, *Letters on the Healing Ministry,* 7–8.

8. Tilda Norberg and Robert D. Webber, *Stretch Out Your Hand* (Cleveland, OH: The Pilgrim Press, 1990), 15.

9. Norman Young, "Healing, Wholeness and the Mystery of Grace," The Sir Alan Walker Lecture, Australia, 1985.

10. George E. Parkinson, *Spiritual Healing* (NY: Hawthorn Books, 1971), 26.

11. *Disciplines* (Nashville, TN: Upper Room Books, 1982), 49.

12. E. Stanley Jones, *Christian Maturity* (NY-Nashville:Abingdon Press, 1957), 325, 326.

13. For further exploration of inner healing therapy, see Appendix C, "Recommended Resources."

14. James K. Wagner, *Blessed to Be a Blessing* (Nashville, TN: Upper Room Books, 1980), 127–128.

15. Tommy Tyson, "Jesus' Easter Message," *Sharing* (San Antonio, TX: International Order of St. Luke the Physician, April 1988), 20.

16. Reginald Mallett, from a sermon preached at Lake Junaluska, NC, July 27, 1988.

17. Wagner, *Blessed to Be a Blessing,* 88.

18. Robert K. Greenleaf, *Servant Leadership* (NY: Paulist Press, 1977), 36.

19. Paula Ripple, *Growing Strong at Broken Places* (Notre Dame, IN: Ave Maria Press, 1986), 69.

20. James Fenhagen, *Mutual Ministry* (NY: The Seabury Press, 1977), 96–97.

21. Maxie Dunnam, *The Workbook of Intercessory Prayer* (Nashville, TN: Upper Room Books, 1979), 15.

22. John Bunyan, quoted in *A Pocket Prayer Book* (Nashville, TN: Upper Room Books, 1941), 8.

23. Steve Harper, *Praying Through the Lord's Prayer* (Nashville, TN: Upper Room Books, 1992), 59.

24. James Montgomery, "Prayer Is the Soul's Sincere Desire," *The United Methodist Hymnal* (Nashville, TN: United Methodist Publishing House, 1989), 492.

25. Frank B. Stanger, from a lecture given in a conference at Methodist Hospital, Louisville, KY, February 8, 1985.

26. Alice L. Pinto, *The Upper Room* (Nashville, TN: Upper Room Books, July/August 1992), 55.

27. Day, *Letters on the Healing Ministry*, 86–87.

28. Gordon Dalbey, "Recovering Healing Prayer," *The Christian Century*, June 9-16, 1982, 690, 691.

29. Dalbey, "Recovering Healing Prayer," 693.

30. Article from the *United Methodist Reporter* (Dallas, TX: October 30, 1992), written by Debra Ennaco McKnight.

31. Matthew H. Gates, "An Experience in Imaging Prayer."

32. E. Stanley Jones, *How to Pray* (Nashville, TN: Abingdon Press, 1943), 3–4.

33. Norberg and Webber, *Stretch Out Your Hand*, 20.

34. *The United Methodist Book of Worship* (Nashville, TN: The United Methodist Publishing House, 1992), 49–50.

35. Charles de Foucauld, *Meditations of a Hermit* (London-NY: Burns & Oates, Orbis Books, 1981), 55.

36. Wagner, *Blessed to Be a Blessing,* 45–46.

37. Wagner, *Blessed to Be a Blessing*, 48.

38. Day, *Letters on the Healing Ministry*, 79–81.

39. Donald Bartow, *The Healing Service* (Canton, OH: Life Enrichment Publishers, 1976), 15.

40. Francis MacNutt, quoted in the *United Methodist Reporter* (Dallas, TX, August 17, 1979).

41. Arthur Walker, from a paper presented at the "Consultation on Healing Ministry," Nashville, TN, October 28-30, 1986.

42. John Genrich, quoted in *Anna, Jesus Loves You* by James Wagner (Nashville, TN: Upper Room Books, 1985), 32.

43. Bernie S. Siegel, *Peace, Love and Healing* (Harper & Row, 1989), 122.

44. Burton Scott Easton, "The Epistle of James," *The Interpreter's Bible*, Vol.12 (New York-Nashville: Abingdon Press, 1957), 15.

45. Kenneth R. Wade, "What Is the New Age Movement?" *Ministry,* March 1989, 4–7.

46. Wagner, *Blessed to Be a Blessing,* 50–59.

47. Wagner, *Blessed to Be a Blessing*, 58–59.

About the Author

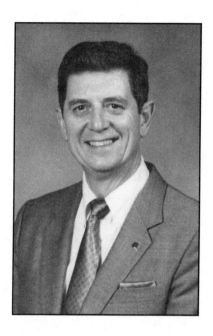

Dr. James K. Wagner became the senior pastor of Fairview United Methodist Church in Dayton, Ohio, in June 1993. Prior to this pastorate, Dr. Wagner joined the staff of The Upper Room in 1984 to serve as the director of The Upper Room Prayer and Healing Ministries and as the executive director of The Disciplined Order of Christ.

Dr. Wagner holds a Doctor of Ministry degree in the area of the Healing Ministry of the Church, as well as the Master of Divinity degree, both from the United Theological Seminary in Dayton, Ohio.

A clergy member of the West Ohio Annual Conference, Dr. Wagner is the author of *Blessed to Be a Blessing* (Upper Room Books, 1980) and *Anna, Jesus Loves You* (Upper Room Books, 1985). He is married to the former Mary Lou Stine, and they have three children: Laurie, Kerrie, and Toby and eight grandchildren.